MW00627411

MACK & JESUS

The Gospel for the Rest of Us

RICK MUMFORD

ISBN: 978-0-578-99082-8

While any stories in this book are true, some names, minor details or identifying information may have been changed to protect the privacy of individuals.

TO AMY

You have been my best friend in ministry and life. We have been through the best and the worst life has to offer, and here we are, still hand in hand, stronger than ever. Thank you for saying yes to this life. And thank you for the way you have been the world's best mom to our three beautiful sons, Mack (left), Cooper (right) and Spencer (front and center).

"Always be prepared to give an answer
to everyone who asks you
to give the reason for the hope that you have.
But do this with gentleness and respect . . ."

1 Peter 3:15

CONTENTS

PREFACE

This is a book about Mack, my firstborn son. And it's a book about Jesus, Mack's creator and best friend. It started out as a therapeutic exercise for me; a way to process loss and grief and memories. Mack & Jesus is what I really want to say to anyone who might be willing to lean in to know about the life of my son and the life of one who loved my son. The story of my son is a part of my story as well, so this book is deeply personal to me on many levels.

I wish everyone could have known Mack. And I believe everyone should have the opportunity to at least know who Jesus is, what He has done, and how He feels about them. But I've noticed that many of us who need Jesus' friendship assume that He wouldn't be interested in us because we are too messed up. God and Jesus and church and religion get lumped into something other people—people who see themselves as good people—do. Many of us know we are not good people, we feel that Jesus wouldn't be interested in us, so we take a hard pass.

In my experience, the Good News of Jesus is often shared in the context of sweet community, belly laughter, zip lines and banana boats. The Gospel is an invitation into a full, rich life of meaning and purpose. But many of us feel too stuck to be welcomed into a community like that. We have secret sin, brokenness, and resentment. If we're honest, life has sucked in some really significant ways. And Jesus? We have tied Him to religion and religion often is, well, ugly. So we walk away from Jesus, not really knowing what and Who we are giving up.

Mack was a beautiful soul, but just as messed up as anyone else. No one really mistook him for a religious guy—he wore all black, had more tattoos than he could count, and smoked cigarettes. Religious people didn't really understand Mack, but lost people flocked to him because they knew they would find unconditional love, grace, and acceptance. And in that context, Mack would introduce them to his Hero and Best Friend.

Mack's story ended abruptly and tragically. But my deep desire is that through these pages, Mack's story will impact your story; that through these pages, he will continue to point people to the One he loved most. Nothing would make me smile more than to know that Mack's life and death helped you draw nearer to his (and my) Savior and Best Friend.

Full disclosure, this book really has nothing to do with macaroni and cheese, though Mack loved it, and I'm guessing Jesus does too. I just thought it was a clever title. This book has everything to do with what life is really all about, and how to find it. Reading it with a bowl of Mac 'n' Cheese is recommended, but a nice cup of coffee would suffice.

1
THE DAY I BECAME A DAD

Right out of college, I married my sweetheart. We had only been married for three years when Amy got pregnant. When the time came for our son to transition out of Amy's womb, I was incredibly nervous. I cried the night before she went into the hospital for a C-section. We had a really good thing going, just the two of us, and I couldn't help but think our little third wheel was going to ruin it.

The next morning, January 10, 1996, Mackenzie Creek Mumford took his first breath of air, and then immediately began screaming at the top of his tiny lungs. I hadn't spent much time with babies, but I was deeply impressed how this tiny mammal could produce such a shrill, piercing sound.

Mack was pink, squirmy, and itty bitty, and I discovered a new kind of love—parental love. This was my son, and my love for him was deep and pure and inexhaustible. I didn't know I had the capacity to love anyone in this way. It was strong, unbreakable, and unconditional. This was my firstborn son.

The hospital asked us to sign discharge papers the next day. Although Amy was still recovering from major surgery, they placed her in a wheelchair and handed her the tiny, squishy human she had miraculously birthed. They wheeled her to the door and wished us the best of luck with the rest of our lives.

Of course, I realize this is a normal series of events. Worldwide, around 385,000 babies are born every day. But I had some concerns. It all felt totally and completely bizarre as I pulled our little blue Ford Escort away from the hospital. Amy was holding her bandaged belly and Baby Mack sat in his backwards-facing car seat. The nurses and doctors had entrusted the two of us with the care of an actual, living human being. What in the world were they thinking? We were ridiculously ill-equipped and way in over our heads.

Yet, the God of the Universe had chosen us for the incredibly special task of being Mack's Mom and Dad. The next 24 years were simultaneously the best and most difficult years of our lives. We absolutely loved being Mack's parents. He was a hilarious toddler and a witty and energetic elementary school kid. We raised him in Kansas, France and California and experienced countless adventures together.

By the time Mack was in middle school, we realized he was making more and more decisions that were contrary to his early training and the standards by which we lived. We thought he was being irresponsible because he was a teenager, because that's what many teens do. But, over time, insecurity, anxiety, poor decision-making and depression, far beyond "typical" teen behaviors, seemed to take control of his thoughts and actions. We struggled to care for him well and he struggled to make sense of what was going on in his brain. But our struggle was together, as a family, rooted firmly in love for God and one another.

In spite of the issues he continually faced, and maybe because of them, Mack went on to serve in various ministries and impact countless people. He was not perfect and he was never free of his mental and emotional struggles. In fact, they increased as he got older. But he had a huge heart of compassion for people—especially broken people. He was sensitive, empathetic and gentle. He was full of wonder, creativity, and was always working on a new idea. He was usually chewing on a toothpick and he had the word "Mom" tattooed in a heart on his right arm. Mack was passionate about coffee, but more passionate about justice. He was servant-hearted, hilarious, and his belly laugh was contagious. God made a one-of-a-kind human and I was proud of the man Mack had become.

2

UNIMAGINABLE GRIEF

On March 26, 2020 I was the Mid-America Regional Director for Young Life. I had to host my monthly regional prayer meeting virtually because the Covid-19 virus was just declared a global pandemic. I thought praying over a video conference call would be awkward, but non-local friends were able to join in and pray with us. We prayed for the next generation, and I prayed specifically for my three sons, Mack, Cooper and Spencer. It was an amazing morning.

The cloudless sky was a brilliant blue, and over the years I cultivated the habit of getting outside on early spring days, just to feel the warm sun on my face and celebrate the fact that I made it through another long, cold Kansas winter. So I pushed aside a few to-do items and meetings that afternoon to play tennis at the park with Oona, our Chinese foreign exchange student, who was living with us that year.

We were still warming up when an Overland Park police cruiser rolled into the parking lot. Two officers got out and began walking directly towards us. Oona and I immediately had the same thought. Were we in trouble? Was it against some sort of ordinance to play tennis because of the Covid-19 virus? What if we got arrested—for playing tennis?

"Rick?" one of the officers called out.

Wait. What? I was perplexed. "Um, did you say my name?" I asked.

"Yes," he said. The two officers slowly walked onto the tennis court. They waited for Oona and me to meet them by the net.

"I'm afraid I have very bad news," he said.

I wasn’t sure how to respond.

“Your son has passed away,” he said quietly.

At first I thought he must be mistaken. Th doesn't even know my family. My mind was swimming. I could sc comprehend the words and was feeling light-headed. My brain see o have gone into vapor lock.

I wondered if he could be talking about Cc Kansas State University had told students to not return to campus Spring Break due to the pandemic, so he was living back at home. v he was running at Shawnee Mission Park that afternoon. Dic et hit by a car? Or was the officer referring to my fifteen-year-old son icer? But I had just seen him right before we left for the park.

I tried to formulate a question. "Which . . " I asked.

"I'm sorry. I don't recall his name," the of eplied. "But he died in Arizona."

Oh no. Mack was in Arizona.

This . . . can't . . . be . . . real. My vision wa ng. I sat down quickly.

I think I began murmuring his name unde reath. "Mack. Oh Mack. Oh no no no Mack."

As a videographer, Mack had been working on a film crew that was shooting a country western movie in Gammons Gulch, a ghost town in Arizona an hour north of Mexico. I had just talked to him a couple of days ago. He was supposed to fly home soon.

"Do you . . . do you know how he died?" d.

The officer paused. He clearly didn't want swer my question. "He took his own life," he said compassionately.

This is the moment my nightmare began. ts say losing a family member to suicide causes catastrophically rauma. Others say the death of a child is the single worst stressor a pers n go through. Now Amy and I were suddenly dealing with both the of a child *and* a suicide simultaneously, alone, during a pandemic.

My sweet firstborn son lived on planet Earth from January 10, 1996 – March 26, 2020. He was here in person for 24 years, 2 months and 17 days.

That's 8,843 days on earth. Every day was a gift, and I got to be Mack's Dad the entire time. I have thought a lot about this little poem by Linda Ellis:

I read of a man who stood to speak
at the funeral of a friend.
He referred to the dates on the tombstone
from the beginning . . . to the end.

He noted that first came the date of birth
and spoke the following date with tears,
but he said what mattered most of all
was the dash between those years.

For that dash represents all the time
that they spent alive on earth.
And now only those who loved them
know what that little line is worth.[1]

If you're reading this book, you are clearly still living in your dash. Your time on earth has begun, but it has not yet ended. That means you still have time to make the most of the days you have left.

---

[1] Linda Ellis, *Live Your Dash: Make Every Moment Matter*. (New York City: Sterling Ethos, 2014).

3

MISSOURI STATE NEWSPAPER CARRIER OF THE YEAR

When I was in elementary school, long before I had ever thought about being someone's Dad, I had a favorite dream. My best nights were when I had my flying dreams. Not flying in an airplane, but just me, banking left and right, feeling the rush of the wind in my face. For some reason I seemed to have trouble keeping my altitude, which concerned me a little, but flapping my arms seemed to help. I don't think I knew where I was headed or why, but I wasn't worried. Everything was awesome because I was flying! Then suddenly the shrill, piercing sound of my alarm clock would jolt me awake like a slap in the face. Why do they have to make alarm clocks so annoying?

As I reached for the snooze button, reality would slowly seep into my consciousness. I wasn't flying. Not even remotely. It was 5:30 a.m. on a bitterly cold Sunday morning and I had to go to work. Every other thirteen-year-old kid I knew would be snug in bed for at least another three hours. But me? I'm a newspaper carrier for the *Columbia Daily Tribune.*

I stumbled awkwardly to the end of my driveway to retrieve the two-foot-tall stack of newspapers, partly because I was still struggling to wake up, and partly because the sub-zero temperatures and strong gusts of wind had made the snow crispy on top. At 115 pounds, I was too heavy to walk on top of the thin, hard layer of snow, but I wasn't heavy enough for my feet to plunge through to the frozen tundra. So my feet would crunch through the top crust, kind of, then it would trip me when I tried to take a step. I eventually managed to get them inside the house.

After rolling and sliding 120 newspapers into individual blue plastic bags, I put them all in my carrier sack—sixty newspapers in front and the other sixty in back. I donned my ski mask, gloves, boots, scarf and carrier sack and plunged out into the darkness. It was 19 degrees below zero outside, but the wind chill made it feel more like negative 50. When the strong winds gusted, I felt like I had forgotten to wear pants.

Just three years earlier, in 1980, the *Empire Strikes Back* came to theaters. Luke Skywalker, though admittedly a bit whiny, was my role model. So I imagined myself to be Luke, stumbling along in the dark on the frozen ice planet of Hoth. My mission was to deliver top secret plans on how to blow up the Death Star to my neighbors, who were all members of the Rebel Alliance. Like Luke, I had little chance of surviving my mission. Hopefully Han Solo would find my near-frozen body and cut open his tauntaun to keep me alive until sunrise.

I delivered newspapers for the *Tribune* every day, 365 days a year. I guess some people somewhere were doing newsworthy things, so the *Tribune* wrote about those people, and apparently every day my Rebel Alliance neighbors wanted to read about them. It was my duty to let the people in my neighborhood know what the newsworthy people were up to.

I got paid 3.2 cents for every newspaper I placed on someone's doorstep. I know that does not sound like much. But after delivering all 120 papers on my paper route, I had made a whopping $3.84—enough for an entire movie ticket. And my job gave me the opportunity to throw nearly 44,000 newspapers a year. Not to brag, but my muscle memory became rather impressive. I learned how to do a back spin so a newspaper would drop perfectly on the Dumas' welcome mat, and a side arm shot to drop the paper just over the Dockweilers' bushes onto their porch. I even learned how to walk the newspaper up the Larsons' front steps and ever-so-gently knock on their front door. Okay, I guess I *am* bragging a little bit.

If one of my neighbors complained about my delivery—their newspaper arrived torn, wet, or late or I accidentally hit their window—the *Tribune* would give me a demerit. But I didn't get many demerits. I was good at my job. In fact, in 1985 I was named the *Columbia Daily Tribune* Newspaper Carrier of the Month. Then I was selected as their Newspaper Carrier of the Year. They took my photo and put my picture in the *Columbia Daily Tribune.* I guess I had become one of the newsworthy people all my neighbors wanted to read about.

All the newspapers across the state of Missouri sent their Newspaper-Carriers-of-the-Year to Jefferson City. My parents made me wear a tie and I sat in a fancy hotel conference room where some very serious grownups asked me questions about my paper route and my goals in life. After lunch, we had our photograph taken with a man named John Ashcroft, who was the state governor. Then, for some reason I will never know (it was probably the tie my Dad tied around my neck) this group of grownups declared me to be the Missouri State Newspaper Carrier of the Year!

A month later I traveled with my parents to the Missouri State Press Association banquet at the Plaza in Kansas City. There, on a large stage, a mustached man with a bulky plaid blazer presented me with a trophy and a $50 U.S. savings bond. My parents explained the $50 bond wouldn't actually be worth cashing in until I was in my mid-thirties, which seemed like a ridiculous award to give a kid. Of course I lost it.

Being the 1985 Missouri State Newspaper Carrier of the Year is a part of my story. It is part of what makes me who I am today, and I am fairly certain that you're not that impressed. You probably haven't ever thought about how newspapers arrived on people's porches in the 1980's. You may not even have ever thought about newspapers at all. And I'm fairly certain you didn't know there used to be a competition in the state of Missouri to determine who the Newspaper Carrier of the Year would be. And now that you do know, I feel confident that you don't care.

And yet this is a part of my story. It's a tiny part of what makes me, me. It's a part of how I see myself—my identity.

I think my paper route taught me the value of hard work and how to manage a tiny paycheck. I think it helped me learn how to save up for something important (like college), helped me to be responsible for my actions, and it may have even contributed to why I still hate freezing cold weather.

Each of us has a story, and every story ma I wonder, what is your story? What are some experiences you hav , good, bad, or just random--that helped make you into the person you oday?

Have you taken time to ask yourself, "Wh ?" I mean, besides your name, gender, age, school, and ethnicity. I ho are you *really*? It's kind of a deep question. But it may be one of tl st important questions we could ever ask ourselves.

But, unfortunately, most of us never do.

Shortly after our second son Cooper was l n 1999, we moved to France. Our little house in Chambourcy h allway with cold tile floors--a perfect place to play Wiggy Waggy. Macl Cooper were just seven and three years old at the time, so I made up a simple game with simple rules. I would throw a super ball as hard as I could down the hall, and it would bounce randomly off the ceiling, floor and walls. Whoever was able to catch the ball got a point. The ball's wild, erratic bouncing off every available surface usually resulted in a pile of giggling boys and a warning from their mother calling from the living room, "No tears! No tears!"

The bouncy ball doesn't know its purpose ourse. It just reacts. It just responds to whatever is in its environmen heading one way and then, wham! A wall! And then it goes another w ham! A ceiling! Many people live their lives like they're in a giant of Wiggy Waggy. They just respond to whatever circumstances come vay. They'll head in some random direction without much thought a en, because someone invited them or said something or did som g, they'll head in another direction for a while.

Here eat this. Um, okay.

You're hot. Do you want to date me? Alright.

Are you going to that party? Um, yeah.

We're protesting something. Okay, let's go.

Wanna play this sport? Sounds fine.

Smoke this. Sure.

There's a job opening here. That'll work I guess.

What if you were to take a step back? Stop bouncing for a few minutes and don't think about what you're going to do next. Instead, take a deep breath, close your eyes and ask yourself, *"Who am I? What makes me, me? How do I see myself? What's my identity?"*

If you draw a blank, don't worry. That's normal. If you have no idea who you are or how to even begin to answer that question, don't worry. There's more to this story.

And there is more to *your* story.

4

WEIRD-O

"Hey Ricky, would you like to go to K-Mart with me?" my Grandpa asked as he handed me a crisp ten-dollar bill. "You can pick out anything you want!"

What?! My mind raced. My Grandpa lived ten hours away in Indiana, so his visit was a special event. And in 1983 ten dollars was three days of paper route wages. The idea of blowing the whole wad on a frivolous shopping trip instead of depositing it into my college fund felt reckless and dangerous. I glanced over to make eye contact with Dad to see what he thought of Grandpa's wild and reckless plan. He just smiled and nodded. Slightly stunned, and carefully holding the treasure with both hands, the two of us hopped in Grandpa's ridiculously large Cadillac.

I considered my options on the drive. I wanted to impress my parents by making a purchase that demonstrated fiscal responsibility. How would a *responsible* thirteen-year-old leverage his ten dollars? Perhaps I should look into investing in something mature like some tools, a book on the stock market, or school supplies. Maybe this was a test, and I should use the money as a down payment to start my own business? But then again, this was a once-in-a-lifetime opportunity to spend money on myself. Grandpa said I could choose *anything I want*!

Near the front entrance of K-Mart, I discovered a giant bin of disheveled shirts on sale. One of the shirts in the bin was an Ocean Pacific® t-shirt. It had a guy surfing a giant wave, a palm tree, and "OP" in the background, like a sunset. This was an obvious choice: all the cool kids at school wore OP shirts with their Levi® 501 red tag button fly jeans, white tube socks and Nike® high top sneakers. I lived in Central Missouri and had never been surfing, but surfers were cool and if my shirt led people to believe I was an amazing surfer it wasn't my fault. This shirt would be my ticket to popularity, fame and success.

The OP shirt was $6, so I still had enough money left over for a second $4 shirt. A graphic on a grey shirt caught my eye. It had the word "Weird-O" written in large block letters across the chest, with a funny face in the 'O'. This had some appeal to me, but it was a gamble: while I want to fit in with everyone and be cool like the kids who were wearing Ocean Pacific, I also want to be my own person.

So, right there in the middle of K-Mart, I began an identity conversation inside my head: *Who am I?* I knew that I definitely wanted to blend in. But I also liked being a little unpredictable and didn't mind that my quirky sense of humor made me stand out a bit. I wouldn't necessarily use the term *Weird-O* to describe myself, but it did speak to my uniqueness. I wanted to be like everyone else, but not *completely* like everyone else. I was cutting edge, wasn't I? Unique. Maybe even a little rebellious. I was, after all, unlike anyone else. I decided to go for it.

The following Monday morning I wore my OP shirt to school, and I am pleased to report that the day went really well. No one said anything about my new shirt. But that's okay, the goal of the OP shirt was to demonstrate how well I fit in. I felt confident my cool-factor was somehow penetrating their subconscious. Mission accomplished.

On Tuesday I summoned up the courage to put on my Weird-O shirt and I walked to the bus stop. Bus #5 picked up both junior high and high school kids from our neighborhood, then dropped off the junior high kids on the way to the high school. Naturally, the high school kids sat in the back.

When my bus pulled up, I walked up the stairs past the driver and around the corner to the yellow line. This brief moment in time is when all the kids already on the bus look up to see who is getting on. You're on stage for everyone to see. It was the first time the world would be exposed to the bold, fun, outside-the-box me, and it was that moment when a high school kid in the back yelled, "Weird-O? You actually put it on your shirt?!" And then everyone on the bus laughed.

I quickly found a seat by myself and sat down. How could I have been so stupid? I gambled, and I lost. Now I had to walk around school all day, proclaiming to everyone that I was weird; I was different; I was an oddball. I was unique, but not in a good way. I was WEIRD. Weird doesn't have a good connotation. Weird means … weird! Why would I advertise this? What was I thinking? I kept my head down all the way to school. I didn't want anyone to notice that the Weird-O had tears in his eyes.

I don't remember that high school kid's name. I don't remember his face, where he lived, or anything about him at all. I'm sure he—and everyone else on the bus—forgot his little joke within fifteen seconds. And yet here I am telling you this story four decades later.

Why? Because I let that experience shape my identity. He called me a Weird-O, and everyone laughed. I assumed they laughed because they all agreed that I was a misfit; that I was an oddball and awkward and I didn't belong. So I became shy. I threw away my Weird-O shirt when I got home from school and only wore my OP shirt. I began to hide the unique, special, quirky part of myself to avoid more pain and ridicule.

You probably think I overreacted. It was just a little joke. All the guy did was read my shirt out loud—and it was *supposed* to be funny. Wasn't that exactly the reaction I was hoping for? And besides, everyone wasn't laughing at me, they were enjoying my shirt. How fragile I must have been, to allow that experience to shape how I saw myself. I should never have let that random kid define my identity.

But we all do this. All the time. We allow what other people say to shape how we see ourselves.

I watched Mack try to figure out his identity. By the time he was four years old, Mack was Batman. He didn't just dress like Batman, he really thought of himself as Batman. This was only reinforced by the Parisians we would pass on the street on our way to market. "Oh la la! Bonjour Batman!" they would say. And he would just nod confidently and reply, "Bonjour."

When we moved from Paris to Los Angel ck took on a surfer identity. Then soon after, he became a chess player s teen years he tried being emo, a hard core rock guy, a skater, and e lly he became a monochromatic guy who didn't wear anyt ut black and white.

We all do this. We bounce around, trying re out who we are. Some of our identity is based on our family of origi r last name, nationality, ethnicity, DNA, genes and native language ll a part of who we are. We are born with some characteristics that hel ne how we see ourselves.

But a lot of our identity is based on what eople say about us. Sometimes people say positive things. The us cute, or smart, or athletic, or creative or tell us we play well thers. We absorb this feedback and it becomes a part of how we urselves.

For instance, if a cute guy tells a girl she's he may smile and say thank you, but she doesn't forget that comment diately. There is a strong possibility that it will subconsciously impa identity. She will likely begin to adjust her activities, friend group, es, wardrobe and social media posts to confirm this identity. As sh ns to identify as a sexy person, it changes her behavior to fit how es herself. She begins to do more and more things she thinks a sexy gi ld do.

If someone tells a guy he's good at footbal 's a nice compliment. Chances are, he'll be more likely to subcon sly see himself as a football player, both on and off the field. He will li egin to adjust his activities, friend group, choices, wardrobe and social a to confirm this identity. As he begins to identify as a football playe anges his behavior. He begins to do more and more things he thi ootball player should do.

But sometimes people say negative things. call us slow, unattractive, unimportant, or they tell us that we don't . We absorb these negative experiences too—even more than the posi xperiences—and it also becomes a part of how we see ourselves.

For instance, if someone tells a girl she's u ere is a good chance that this comment will impact her identity. She kely begin to adjust her activities, friend group, choices, wardrobe cial media to confirm this identity. As she begins to identify as an ugly person, it changes her behavior.

We all make our decisions and choices based on who we perceive ourselves to be. Our identity impacts how hard we try in school, who we hang around with, who we sit by at lunch, how we spend our time, what we wear, what we drink, who we date, where we work, what sports we play, how much effort we put into those sports, whether or not we go to college, and what we post online. And much of our identity is determined by what other people say about--and do to--us. Our identity is often formed in adolescence, and it can set the trajectory for the rest of our lives.

If we get pulled over for speeding, the police officer asks for our *identification.* Identification is what others say *about* us. The State identifies us by our legal names, DMV photo and driver's license number. In contrast, *identity* is how we see ourselves.

Here's the rub. We can run into trouble when we let identification (what others say about us) define our identity (how we see ourselves) because humans do not have the right or authority to define other humans' identities.

Someone can call you stupid or smart, mean or kind, greedy or generous, ugly or handsome, racist or welcoming, strong or weak, normal or weird-o if they like. Clearly people talk about other people all the time. But what they say about you doesn't need to impact how you see yourself—because they're just human, like you. They do not have the right to define you.

What someone says about someone else can be interesting or sometimes even helpful. But you were created by a Creator. God decided the world would be incomplete without a . . . you. He designed you, knit you together, and put you on this planet. The goal is not to build your identity only on the positive feedback you get from other people. The real question is this: What does your Creator say about you?

Perhaps you would tell me that I am kind. Thank you. I hope that is true about me. In fact, there are many things you could point out that are true about me. I'm also a bald American who wears jeans and glasses and enjoys Cracker Barrel fried chicken on my birthday, which is August 2nd. These are all true statements about me. But only my Creator can tell me what is *most* true about me.

In the same way, there are many things that are true about you, but only your Creator can tell you what is *most* true about you. Ultimately, He is the only one who has a right to speak into your identity—how you see yourself. His voice matters most.

So what does God say about you?

5
SO WONDERFULLY MADE IT'S DOWNRIGHT SCARY

Before Amy and I had children, I went to graduate school in Denver. An imposing stone building was located just a few miles from our small apartment. Every weekday, people gathered in that building to produce little copper plated zinc coins called pennies. They literally produced money there, and no one tried to stop them. It was totally legal.

People today argue about race, politics, laws, ethics, equality, and pretty much everything there is to have an opinion about. Many people seem to be angry with other people about something most of the time. Wouldn't it be remarkable if we could find something that all Americans could agree on? Would you believe there actually is something? Amazingly, everyone has agreed that the people in this building on Colfax Avenue in Denver can use machines to crank out little bronze-colored coins and declare their value at $1/100^{th}$ of a dollar.

Every store accepts these pennies as currency. If I am able to collect enough of them, I can trade pennies for a burger, a 4K television, or even my own jet airplane.

Imagine you were to take a field trip to the Denver Mint and you buy a brand new, bright, shiny, clean penny from the gift shop. As you are walking to your car admiring your new treasure, gleaming brightly in the sunlight, you notice another penny in the parking lot. You pick it up and notice it has been worn down from years of use. It's gunky, grimy and sticky and hardly recognizable as a penny. Who knows how many bacteria colonies are living on this nasty coin from 1972? You hold the two coins, side-by-side, in the palm of your hand before putting them in your pocket and reaching for the hand sanitizer.

What is the value of the shiny, brand new, beautiful, freshly-minted penny? Its value is one cent, that's easy. So what is the value of the nasty, germ-infested, worn-down penny? Its value is also one cent! How can this be? Because the value of these coins is determined by their creator. The U.S. government made them, and the government says they're both worth one cent. The physical appearance of the coin doesn't impact the penny's value--not even one little bit.

The Ford Motor Company makes a truck they call the F-150. Ford set the suggested retail price of this year's base model at $28,745. What right does Ford have to set the price of this truck? Actually, they have every right, because the value of this truck is determined by its maker. You or I may have opinions about the value of the F-150, but, honestly, our opinions don't matter. We can say whatever we want, but Ford created the truck and if Ford declares the F-150 MSRP to be $28,745, that *is* the value.

If you were to write a song that a musician wanted to purchase and record, she would ask you how much money you want for it. As the creator, you get to determine the song's value. If you were to create a painting that an art collector wanted to hang in her gallery, she would ask you how much money you would accept for it because it is your creation. As the creator, you get to determine the painting's value.

Just like the penny, the truck, the song and the painting, *you* have a Creator. You did not create yourself or decide to be born. You never thought, "Hmm, I think I'd like to go to Earth and see what it's like to be a carbon-based life form." You had no thoughts at all until you were created because you are God's choice, His creation. And, as your Creator, He determines your value.

There are many things that are true about you, but only your Creator gets to determine your true value. Other people may try to weigh in, and you may be tempted to allow their words and actions to impact how you see yourself. But ultimately, their opinions don't matter.

So the million-penny question is: *What does God say about your worth?*

God tells us in the Bible that you were made in His image[2]. He knows literally everything about you and He is familiar with all your ways[3]. Even the very hairs on your head are numbered![4]

God says He knew you even before you were conceived, so you are not a mistake. He decided the world needed you, exactly you. He knit you together in your mother's womb[5] and determined the exact time of your birth and where you would live.[6] He says His desire is to lavish His love on you,[7] for you are His treasured possession!

And He also says that you are fearfully and wonderfully made[8].

You are *fearfully* made. That means He created you with great reverence, heart-felt interest, and with respect. In a way, God is saying that you are so wonderfully made it's downright scary! The more scientists and doctors learn about the human body, the more impressed they are with the way God designed you and me.

He also says you are *wonderfully* made. The God who made you stepped back from His work of art, folded His arms and smiled. When He looked at you, His creation, He liked what He saw. He thinks you have inestimable value. Many of us look in the mirror and see flaws. We think we are too short or tall, too fat or skinny, too light or dark, too hairy or bald, too young or old, too dumb, too clumsy, or too impaired. We think our nose is too big, our ears are too wrinkled, and our teeth are too crooked. But God thinks you are wonderfully made. You are unique. You are set apart. You are special, just the way you are.

---

[2] Genesis 1:27

[3] Psalm 139:3

[4] Luke 12:7

[5] Psalm 139:13-14

[6] Acts 17:26

[7] 1 John 3:1

[8] Psalm 139:14

Did you know that when light hits your ey tiny cells in some tissue at the back of your eye somehow turn that li; o electrical signals? It seems dangerous to have electrical signals your head, but God trained those signals to run up a nerve to your bra en your brain magically transforms those signals into images, so yc see. I have no idea how the squishy, moist lump known as your brain i to convert electrical signals into images. But it does, and you can now ive color, shape, form, light, distance, and perspective in 3-D. I don't u and how this works, yet God designed eyesight and most of us get perience it firsthand. We are fearfully and wonderfully made!

Did you know that about 96 million of the in your body are going to die in the next minute? That seems super ght? But don't panic. By the time that minute is up, about 96 million ce l have divided, replacing those that died. You are constantly being r new! You are fearfully and wonderfully made!

Or think about your blood vessels for a se (which is probably something no one has ever asked you to d you were to pull them out of your body and stretch them out into a s t line, that would be super gross. But it would also be 100,000 miles l That is like traveling around the entire world nearly four times. I have r a how God packed 100,000 miles of blood vessels in you. It seems like vould be more bloated than you are. But this is what He has done. Yo earfully and wonderfully made!

We have hours and hours of very boring home video footage of Mack as a baby. He would literally do nothing but lay on his back and I would just let the video camera roll—caught up in awe and wonder of the shockingly beautiful bundle God created when He created my boy. I'm thankful for these videotapes now.

I could go on and on about the complexity awesomeness of your skin, heart, brain, digestive system, nose, lungs, muscles and bones, but then this book would become a biology book, and plenty of those have already been written. So let me get to the point: only your Creator can tell you what is *most* true about you. Only He gets to determine your true value. He says you are fearfully and wonderfully made. And so you are.

Your Creator knows everything about you. He is the expert on who you truly are, and His opinion is the only one that matters. The truest thing about God is what He says about Himself. The truest thing about you is what He says about you. And I have it on good authority that He thinks you're awesome.

6
THADDEUS' INVENTION

Mack had a dog named George. Mack loved George very much and wanted to take him everywhere, and George loved Mack and wanted to go everywhere. But George was a Pomeranian spaz. It was dangerous to have George loose in the car, but he hated being confined to a box in the back seat.

Mack was incredibly creative and innovative, so he designed and invented a car seat for George that was attached to the middle console between the front seats. George was delighted to sit right next to Mack, see out, not get tangled up in his leash, and Mack could drive safely. Ingenious!

I want to tell you a parable about another inventor. Once upon a time in a land far, far away, there was an inventor named Thaddeus. At the young age of twenty, Thaddeus quit his barista job and began working on what he hoped would be the world's greatest invention. For the next sixty years, Thaddeus labored every day in his warehouse—researching, developing, designing and building. He invested millions of dollars on his masterpiece. He never went out on a date and never married because he didn't want a family to interfere with his life's work. Thaddeus did not have friends or hobbies. He never took a vacation, never enjoyed a worship service, and never played sports. Instead, he was entirely focused, committed, and invested in his one goal, the completion of his ultimate achievement: the world's greatest invention.

At last, as a tired elderly man, hunched over Thaddeus put the finishing touches on his massive machine. He held a giant press conference and invited the public into his warehouse. Hundreds of reporters and curious people came from all around the state with television cameras and smartphones to document the historic moment.

Thaddeus smiled as he walked to the stage he built. "This is it!" he thought to himself. "This is the moment I have worked towards my entire life." He delivered a marvelous speech about how much time, energy, effort, creativity, ingenuity, design and money it took to create his masterpiece. And then he walked over to the machine and drew in a deep breath.

As he pulled the giant sheet off of the invention, the crowd gasped. They couldn't help but marvel! It had knobs and tubes, latches and levers; giant bronze bells and glowing electronic screens. It had incorporated all of the latest computer technology and looked like something from another world. The creativity and beauty of the sleek yet intricate design was absolutely spectacular. It was modern, complicated, beautiful and incredibly complex.

"Are you ready for me to turn it on?" Thaddeus asked the crowd.

"Yes!" they replied.

"I said, are you READY?" Thaddeus asked again for dramatic effect.

"YES!" the crowd bellowed in unison. Then, with a tear in his eye, Thaddeus dramatically flipped on the master power switch. Without a moment's hesitation, it began to whirl to life. It shook and hummed. The crowd could hear various elements and processes beginning to come to life within the machine. It was working perfectly!

After savoring the moment, Thaddeus slowly turned his back to the machine and walked back on stage to the microphone. "I will now be happy to answer your questions," he smiled. Hands immediately shot up everywhere. "Yes," Thaddeus said, "the young lady there in the front row.

What is your question?"

"Yes, thank you," the young reporter said. "Your invention is so complex and intricate. Clearly it has been fearfully and wonderfully made! What, exactly, does it do?"

"Hmm," thought Thaddeus, stumped. "I'm not exactly sure. I hadn't really thought of that. I don't know that my invention really *does* anything at all."

There was an awkward pause in the room. All the hands went down and there were no more questions. The crowd slowly dispersed, confused and disappointed, murmuring to one another. The event didn't make the local news. There is nothing remarkable about an invention that doesn't have a purpose.

Yes, my made-up story is ridiculous. Aren't all inventions supposed to have a purpose? Make the world a better place? Meet some sort of need? But do you know what is even more ridiculous? The idea that God would create *you* without a purpose.

Do you think God would have created you such value, beauty, intricate design and wonder and not given you a purpose? You are a million times more complex and wonderful than anything the world's greatest inventors could create, and God made you this way for a reason. You were designed on purpose for a purpose. You are His masterpiece, the pinnacle of His creation, but His intent wasn't for you to just sit there and be fearfully and wonderfully made.

A toaster is a relatively simple invention, especially when compared to Thaddaeus' wonderfully complex machine. Put the bread in, push the lever down, and the electric current flowing through the thin filaments create a steady supply of heat that toasts the whole bread surface. That's what the toaster does. That is its purpose. That is why it is called a 'toast-*ER*.'

Let's say you wanted to play soccer with friends and couldn't find your soccer ball. The toaster would make a poor substitute. Using a toaster as a soccer ball wouldn't go well for the toaster, and it wouldn't go well for your foot. You'd undoubtedly destroy the toaster, and kicking metal is typically a bad idea. The toaster performs best when it is used to, well, toast things.

Don't get me wrong. Toasters are cool. I'r anti-toaster. But to be honest your toaster would perform poorly ›ar of soap, a sweater, a lawn mower or an iPad. If you tried to use ›aster as a pencil sharpener, you might get angry at the toaster. You mi ll the toaster that it is stupid and that it is the worst toaster ever. And if ›aster had feelings, it may believe you and allow your words to impa‹ way it feels about itself. Your harsh words may cause the poor littl ter to have low self-esteem and think of itself as worthless.

But the toaster was carefully designed and ›d by someone who set out to make a specific appliance for a specific ›se. The toaster-creator did not concern himself as to whether it could ıce or sharpen pencils. In fact, he even wrote an instruction manual ıcluded it with the toaster so you could get the most out of your small a ıce.

It's amazing how many people, fearfully ar nderfully made by God, are walking around having no idea why they w ›eated. They don't know their purpose. They just bounce as if they n one giant game of Wiggy Waggy (see chapter three).

Think about it. No one sets a goal to beco ı alcoholic. Someone just invites them to have a drink, so they do. A en they do it again. And then it becomes a thing they just do. And ı 's a thing they do a little more. And then, eventually, something the d to do becomes something that is done to them.

I once went to a funeral for an elderly mar died of cancer. Like you, he was fearfully and wonderfully made in the : of God. But his funeral felt awkward because no one really knew v ɔ say. He was a manager in a company, played golf, told some jokes, a ıtched television. He did stuff, but his purpose was unclear to him ɛ everyone else, and then he was gone.

God is really excited about His creation. F de you, so if He thinks you're amazing, you *are* amazing! He creat‹ ı *with a purpose.* He has a plan for you, a mission for you. You are n‹ taking up space. You're not here to just bounce. You have a role t‹ that is infinitely more important than making toast!

Wouldn't it be wonderful to do more than just bounce your way through life? Wouldn't it be delightful to know your purpose and live it out? But can you ever know your purpose?

$$\hat{H}_{WdW}\Psi := "\frac{1}{\sqrt{G}}\frac{\delta}{\delta h^{ab}}\left\{\sqrt{g}\,G^{abcd}\frac{\partial\Psi}{\delta h^{cd}}\right\} - \xi\, Ric(h;G)"\,\Psi - \sqrt{h}\,Ric(x;h)\,\Psi + \sqrt{h}\,2\Lambda\Psi + \hat{H}^{matter}_{WdW}\Psi = \emptyset$$

7

LIFE TO THE FULL

There are some inventions, like the toaster, I might be almost smart enough to understand. Although I would have difficulty building my own toaster from scrap pieces of metal, I am pretty sure I can wrap my brain around *how* a toaster works. It feels fairly straight forward.

When we lived in Europe in the early 2000s, I met a Young Life volunteer leader in Geneva who worked for Cern, a company that had the world's largest and most powerful particle accelerator. It consisted of a 17-mile ring of superconducting magnets with a number of accelerating structures to boost the energy of the particles along the way. My conversation with Simon was strange. "How was work today, Simon?"

"Well, actually," he replied, "today we had the particle accelerator in a tandem configuration, so it accelerated singly charged negative ions to high energies where they were stripped of electrons in a foil cell. In the case of some radionuclides (like 10Be), the BeO− ion was injected. Naturally, this made the energy calculation more complex, since we had to account for the breakup of the molecular species in the stripper canal. So yeah, charged positive ions that resulted from this interaction were further accelerated back to ground potential."

"Cool. So you had a good day then?"

As it turns out, particle accelerators are way more complicated than toasters. Simon had a Ph.D. in Particle Physics and had spent his life studying this stuff so he was able to comprehend what particles were and what might happen when they accelerate. Because he had context, he could understand the value and purpose of a particle accelerator.

You are infinitely more wonderfully and fearfully designed than a particle accelerator. Just as Simon needed to understand advanced physics before he could know the purpose of a particle accelerator, you are going to need to understand your own context before you can truly understand your purpose in life.

Many people skip this process. They don't ever stop to explore why they were created. So they just assume their function is to play sports, make money and/or babies, or consume resources. They just bounce. But they were made for so much more!

The first step to understanding your context is to look to your Creator. Who made you?

The book of John in the Bible begins with a poetic introduction to Jesus. John calls Jesus "The Word." It goes like this:

> *"In the beginning was the Word, and the Word was with God, and the Word was God. He was with God in the beginning. Through him all things were made; without him nothing was made that has been made. In him was life, and that life was the light of all mankind."*[9]

Since Jesus is "the Word," let's just insert His name into this verse. It will be a little less poetic, but I want to make sure this is crystal clear:

> *"In the beginning was Jesus, and Jesus was with God, and Jesus was God. Jesus was with God in the beginning. Through Jesus all things were made; without Jesus nothing was made that has been made. In Jesus was life, and that life was the light of all mankind."*

Just so we're all on the same page:

1. Jesus is God.
2. You exist because Jesus made you.
3. All life, including yours, comes from Jesus.

Fortunately for us, we don't have to sit around and wonder what Jesus, our Creator, is like. He actually made a very intentional decision to enter into

---

[9] John 1:1-3

our time-space continuum about 2,000 years ago. John continues in verse 14:

> *"The Word became flesh and made his dwelling among us. We have seen his glory, the glory of the one and only Son, who came from the Father, full of grace and truth."*[10]

Jesus created Earth, and then inserted Himself into history! We have a historical record of what He said and did while He was visiting His creation. This is really wonderful news because now we don't have to wonder about what our Creator is like. The book of Colossians says that Jesus is the image of the invisible God[11]. Although you can't see God, Jesus was alive and in-person. By looking at Jesus, you can see what God is like. And if you have access to a Bible, you can read for yourself what Jesus said and did.

Actually, would you mind if we were to open up the Bible and take a peek at the day in the life of Jesus right now?

Let's flip over a few pages in the book of John to chapter 10. Here we find Jesus talking to the religious leaders of the day (called "Pharisees"). Imagine a group of Middle Eastern guys standing around in their togas and sandals, chatting. You can recognize the Pharisees by their fancy religious outfits (notice the little boxes of scripture strapped to their left arms and extra-long fringes on their garments). Jesus is wearing a simple outfit, talking to them about the people who will follow and put their trust in Him. He was using a figure of speech to compare His followers to sheep:

> *"Very truly I tell you, I am the gate for the sheep. All who have come before me are thieves and robbers, but the sheep have not listened to them. I am the gate; whoever enters through me will be saved. They will come in and go out, and find pasture. The thief comes only to steal and kill and destroy; I have come that they may have life, and have it to the full."*[12]

People use this phrase that Jesus coined, "life to the full," to mean all sorts of things. Sometimes people use it to describe their white water rafting trip, getting super drunk, or working overtime. But what did *Jesus* mean when he

---

[10] John 1:14
[11] Colossians 1:15
[12] John 10:7-10

used this phrase?

We already know that Jesus gave life. The ;ees didn't realize it, but the only reason they were alive in the first plac ecause Jesus had given them life. Jesus was the reason why their h were beating and they had activity in their brain stems. But Jesus was ; His purpose in coming to earth was to bring *life to the full.* That's mor ı just being physically alive.

Jesus is speaking to our universal desire fo llment. Deep down we all want to thrive, not just merely survive. Wε to live full lives, not just simply exist. We were created with the abil feel emotions and the hunger to grow and learn because we were ed by God in His own image. So we try to grasp onto every expeı , soak up every relationship, and maximize every opportunity. Yet even strive to fill our lives to the brim with pleasure, wealth, excitement, po nd adventure, we are never fully satisfied.

A number of years ago, when Tom Brady on "just" three Super Bowls (he now has seven), he mused durir nterview about his success. "Why do I have three Super Bowl rings an think there's something greater out there for me?" Tom wondered l. "I mean, maybe a lot of people would say, 'Hey man, this is what iı reached my goal, my dream, my life. Me, I think, 'God, it's got t nore than this.' I mean this isn't, this can't be what it's all cracked up t '

The interviewer asked Tom, "What's the a ?"

Brady replied, "I wish I knew. I wish I kne ɔve playing football and I love being quarterback for this team. But a same time, I think there are a lot of other parts about me that I'm tryir ind."[13]

God created many things that we can enjo , for one of the greatest quarterbacks of all time, one of those thin ɔotball. But football can't give life to the full. Nothing God created c tisfy this hunger. No circumstance, no matter how remarkable a nazing, will truly meet our

---

[13] Daniel Schorn, "Transcript: Tom Brady Tall ceve Kroft, Part 3," 60 Minutes, November 4, 2005. https://www.cbs :om/news/transcript-tom-brady-part-3/

deepest hunger for life to the fullest. And no circumstance, no matter how terrible, needs to snatch it away.

One of the perks of being on Young Life staff is doing a summer assignment at Young Life camp. I would go for a month to serve as the Camp Speaker at Young Life's Castaway Club near Detroit Lakes, Minnesota. My family would go with me to relax, play and serve at the camp in various ways.

One summer when Mack was middle school age, he was really struggling. He was making poor decisions and not living life to the full. He had begun to self-harm and we were concerned for his health and safety. Mack was deeply frustrated with himself. He felt messed up and broken and he wasn't really sure why. He sat in the back of our minivan with headphones in all the way to Castaway.

We learned that there were not enough beds where the family was staying. So he wouldn't have to sleep on the floor, Mack found an available bed in a bunk room where a friend named Paul was staying. Paul was a professional drummer, but, more than that, he had a vibrant relationship with Jesus. During the month we were at camp, Paul stayed up late night after night, listening to Mack, caring for him, accepting him and loving him. Mack felt incredibly seen and heard and understood by Paul. By the end of the month, Mack was able to fully embrace the reality that he was also seen and heard and understood by Jesus. Though Mack had made a profession of faith and been baptized a few years earlier, this was undoubtedly a turning point in his life. He really embraced his relationship with Jesus; he came back from camp changed, renewed and refreshed. It's like the light in his heart had been turned on again.

Jesus came to offer a full spiritual life that's not based on the things of this world. Life is more than entertainment, comfort, gratifying our desires and even winning the Super Bowl. Jesus tried to help the religious leaders understand that this life lived to the fullest is a life that is characterized by one thing—a relationship with Jesus Himself. Jesus was saying that direction, meaning, contentment, truth, joy, peace, and purpose are found in Himself. In fact, it's the very reason why He came.

Either Jesus was just making up stuff to try to impress the religious guys, or there is truth to His claim. Either way, we should probably find out.

8

FIRST IMPRESSIONS

In college, I lived with an incredible group of Christian guys in a run-down house called the "Dude's Ranch." We would throw dance parties, play late night Skip-Bo®, host Bible studies and have marshmallow wars. A marshmallow war, by the way, is an activity I highly recommend if you don't care about breaking things in your house. Simply place a bag of very stale marshmallows in the middle of the floor and, at the signal, throw them as hard as you can at your roommates. Whoever has the most welts when the bag is empty is the loser. It's honestly more fun than it sounds.

One day a stray kitten began hanging around the Dude's Ranch. It was lost and hungry, so I fed the little thing. Not surprisingly, the kitten stuck around. I named it Haggai after a random Old Testament prophet because I thought it was funny. Later, I learned that Haggai was a girl-cat and not a boy-cat, which only made her name funnier. Haggai (the cat, not the prophet) was a cool, laid-back fuzzy friend and I became quite fond of her. Haggai even learned to do some tricks and when I'd hold her up upside down near the ceiling she could capture mosquitos in her paws.

One night I walked in from night class and all four of my roommates were sitting quietly in the living room. They weren't watching television. No one was talking or studying or writing a paper. They were just sitting there, stone quiet. I knew immediately something was wrong, and stopped just inside the front door, puzzled. Mark, our most mature roommate, looked at me soberly and seriously.

"Rick, we have something we need to tell you," he said. "It's about Haggai."

I set down my book bag and slowly slid onto the couch. I drew in a deep breath and began to prepare myself for the worst.

"We were having a marshmallow war," Mark began. I didn't anticipate that being the first phrase to come out of Mark's mouth. "And, well, you see," Mark stammered, "one of the marshmallows hit Haggai in the eye. Rick, I'm so sorry!"

"So," I asked, "she's alive?"

"Oh yes," Mark smiled, "but she was squinting." Mere moments later Haggai happily sauntered around the corner and into the living room, happy as a clam. And she wasn't even squinting.

I had braced myself for the absolute worst. I thought perhaps someone had called the house phone while I was at class and told my roommates there had been a terrible accident. Perhaps there had been a death in my family or some other life-altering tragedy. But, in reality, my cat got hit by a marshmallow and had squinted for a few minutes. Thankfully, my first impression of what I feared might be true was way off.

Have you ever experienced that? Have you ever done a double-take? You thought you saw your Uncle Gene at Target but then looked again and realized it's just another bald guy?

As I mentioned in the previous chapter, Jesus claimed to have arrived on the very planet He had breathed into existence for the purpose of bringing people "life to the full." And I realize that as soon as I mention the name of Jesus, a preconceived notion of who He is immediately pops into your head.

We taught Mack about Jesus from the earliest age. When he was just two years old, Amy went to get him out of his crib after his afternoon nap. "Hi

Mommy!" he chirped. Then he looked up at the ceiling, waved and called out, "Hi Jesus!"

When he was three, Mack shared some theology with his babysitter, "God is my Father, and is a very, very tall man. And He works with Jesus." I mean, sure. Kind of.

Whether or not you grew up in a Christian home, Jesus remains the most famous, planet-altering person to walk the face of the earth. Beyond the fact that today's calendar date is based on His arrival, Jesus has had a profound impact on culture, social systems, law, education, health care, charity, and the arts. You've heard his name countless times. So when I mention the name of Jesus—what image pops into your head?

Some people think of Jesus as a myth or a character from an old story, like the Greek hero Odysseus in *The Odyssey* by Homer. They say Jesus was just a legend that religious people like to talk about.

Other people think of Jesus as a type of genie. He's like an imaginary friend that you can call out to when you didn't study and you need an A on the Geometry exam. Just close your eyes and wish for what you want, and maybe He'll bring you good luck. He's kind of like a skinny version of Santa Claus without the red suit, available to grant your wishes year-round.

Some have been conditioned to think of a Renaissance Jesus. The paintings we see in art galleries make him look like a sad, exhausted, serious and boring white guy. He's got a cool religious design screen-printed on the front of a gold-hemmed robe and he's low-key flashing a peace sign with His right hand. And for some inexplicable reason, the back of his head appears to be glowing. He looks very religious and completely unapproachable.

Some think of Jesus as a skinny, homeless wimp who walked around barefoot and jobless, and hung out with sick people and sinners. He was basically a hippie who accepted everyone, got along with everyone, ignored people's sin altogether, and was fond of th tles' song, "All You Need is Love."

Others are like Ricky Bobby in the scene f he movie *Talladega Nights* who prefers to think of God as an eight-p six-ounce newborn baby Jesus. Before he eats his KFC, Ricky want lk to a Jesus who is cuddly yet omnipotent.

I have met a lot of people who think of Je the Ultimate Religion Guy because we mostly think and talk about Je church—and church is where religion is. So, we associate what we arned from the modern American version of church (dull sermons s shoes, stained glass windows, and moldy song books) and assu at must be what Jesus is into.

Unfortunately, many people today are gett eir theology from two-sentence social media posts by people that st pulling ideas out of a hat. There are no rules about what a person ca online about Jesus, so literally anyone can twist Jesus' words or i o fit whatever agenda they are trying to push. Then others chime in w eir ideas . . . and on and on it goes. Sometimes there is even a poll to c ine whether people agree with what the first person posted. Some p claim that Jesus didn't exist, while others say He was a racist. Son m Jesus condones sexual sin and others say He never claimed to be n the flesh. Most of us aren't familiar enough with the historical a ts of what Jesus actually said and did to separate the truth from the o they tend to just roll with what appears to be the most popular view.

But truth is only truth when it agrees with r reality. Let's say all your friends and family got together and decide elieve Jesus co-founded Chick-Fil-A with S. Truett Cathy. Your vi nt, no matter how strongly and sincerely you hold to it, would have a ely no bearing on reality. Bottom line: you'd be wrong. Truth is not ever you decide it to be. Truth is whatever is true.

So it would be wise to consider that it is at within the realm of possibility that your first impression of Jes ght be wrong. If you were to sit down and read the historical record i thew, Mark, Luke or John, you would be able to see what Jesus actual l and did, and learn what

He meant when He claimed to have come to bring life to the full. What you'll discover is that Jesus is the most amazing person to ever walk the face of the earth. I think you'll realize that Jesus is everything you want most--wonderful, attractive, strong, gracious, and loving, beyond any other person this world has ever seen.

The interesting thing is that, in Biblical days, not everyone liked Jesus. Not everyone was a fan.

In fact, a quick scroll through social media will tell you that people are divided about Him even to this day. So it seems the next thing we need to do is open the Bible together and take a closer look at this man who claimed to bring life to the full.

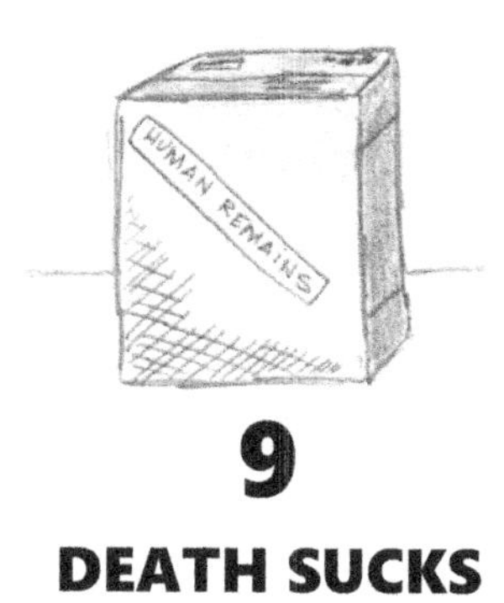

9
DEATH SUCKS

After learning of Mack's death, I crawled into the back of the police cruiser, stunned and dizzy. They drove Oona and I back home, where I saw my sweet wife standing on the driveway. When I saw her face, I knew she already knew. I could tell she was in shock, her eyes full of terror and confusion and love. She was the one who had sent the police to come find us. We melted into one another's arms.

The officers said something about letting them know if we needed anything else. Then they walked back to their cruiser and drove away, leaving Amy and I completely and hopelessly shattered.

I wanted to call Mack and confirm that this was all a big mistake. I just wanted to hear him laugh and hear his wild explanation for how this was all just a misunderstanding. He was fine, fine, everything was fine.

But everything was not fine.

The next day a friend sent me a YouTube video of a choir singing the hymn, "It is Well with My Soul." If my soul was anything, it certainly wasn't well. My soul was utterly crushed.

Mack was here, alive, breathing, talking, laughing, and eating. Mack loved Jesus and let that love freely spill out to everyone he met. He had a spunky little dog named George and lived in Austin with his wife. He worked on film crews, got tattoos, and fancied big burgers. He chewed on toothpicks, relished deep theological discussions by the bonfire, enjoyed building stuff and listened to Phil Collins on his record player. Then suddenly and dramatically he left my world without saying goodbye, leaving an incomprehensible hole in my heart.

Most days on my commute home from work, Mack and I would talk on the phone. We had become more than father and son, we were best friends. He cared for me deeply, as I cared for him. When I talked to Mack, he made me feel valued and interesting. I enjoyed our conversations immensely. Suddenly my commute home from work was filled with a deafening silence.

Sometimes I still look up Mack's location on the *Find My Friends* app. The jolting response never changes: "No location found."

The fact is—death sucks. Anyone who tells you otherwise has not truly walked through "the valley of the shadow of death."[14]

Jesus, who said He came to bring life to the full, knows that death sucks. In John chapter 11 we read about a day in the life of Jesus. He had some friends who lived in a town called Bethany who were siblings. Their names were Lazarus, Mary and Martha. One day Lazarus became very sick. He got worse and worse, and tragically, Lazarus eventually died from the illness. His family and friends gathered together, heartbroken. Totally devastated and utterly undone by this loss, they wrapped up the dead body, had a funeral, sang songs, spoke fondly of him and wept. Then they placed the corpse in a tomb.

Four days later, Jesus finally arrived in Bethany. Martha heard that Jesus was coming and she went out to meet them. (Jesus and Martha had a really interesting conversation that I will come back to in a bit). When Mary saw Jesus, she fell at his feet sobbing and said, "Lord, if you had been here, my

---

[14] Psalm 23:4 NASB

brother would not have died."[15]

When Jesus saw her weeping, and the Jews who had come along with her also weeping, he was deeply moved in spirit and troubled. "Where have you laid him?" he asked.

"Come and see, Lord," they replied.

Jesus wept. Then the Jews said, "See how he loved him!"

I've heard some theologians discuss the reasons why they think Jesus chose to weep. I don't think it's really all that complicated. Jesus, who had come to bring life to the full, saw the anguish, pain, heartbreak and devastation the loss of a loved one brings, He felt it deeply and wept alongside His friends. Death sucks. Jesus felt grief, and he cried.

Somehow it helps me to know that Jesus wept. He identified with Mary and Martha's heart-wrenching grief. And Jesus understands my grief. Sadness, pain, and heartache are not incompatible with spirituality. It's okay to feel feelings of grief when confronted with the death of a loved one. In fact, God is close to the broken-hearted[16] and the poor in spirit are blessed[17] in a tender and special way. But Lazarus' death is not the end of the story.

Jesus walked with his friends until he arrived at the tomb with Mary and Martha and all the people who were together there mourning. He saw that Lazarus' body had been laid to rest in a cave with a stone barring the entrance. Now here's where the story takes a twist. Jesus said "Take away the stone."

"But, Lord," said Martha, the sister of the dead man, "by this time there is a bad odor, for he has been there four days."

Martha is offering very solid advice. Lazarus was dead, and there was simply no coming back from that. When something that is alive is cut off from its source of life, it deteriorates. If you snip a beautiful flower, it won't be beautiful in three days. Once a living creature's heart and brain and organs

---

[15] John 11:21

[16] Psalm 34:18

[17] Matthew 5:3

cease to function, it decays.

This is why exhuming a dead body from a is nasty business. Lazarus was as dead as a squirrel that was squished ıe highway a week ago. He was as dead as a mouse, caught in a mouse wrapped in a plastic grocery sack and taken out with the trash l onth. I'm not trying to be gross. The reality is that death is gross. Mc us have few experiences with death. We don't think about it often, hen real death occurs, everything stops working and the decomp n process begins. A dead body, even if it is a loved one, is not some we are drawn to. We are *supposed* to be appalled, disturbed and deep hered by death. Death reminds us that something is very, very wr ith our existence on this planet. Death was not in God's original pl

But Jesus insisted they roll away the stone, ey did. Then He yelled into the tomb at the corpse of a man who had dead for four days, "Lazarus, come out!"

A few weeks after Mack died, the doorbell Mack was on my front porch. My sweet boy was home. Except, it ust a box plastered with bright yellow tape that read, in bold letters MAN REMAINS." Human remains? As in, the contents of th contained all that remained of my human?

With tears in my eyes and a lump in my th picked up the box and took it to the garage, where I opened it wi ility knife. I know it sounds crazy, but I was careful with the knife. I gu was gentle because my son's body was inside that box, and I woul er want to hurt my son. Inside the cardboard box was another box this one was black. It was much heavier than I expected, though it w s heavy as Mack was when he came home a few months earlier to cel Christmas. I quietly slipped Mack's cremated remains in a cabinet in th ıg room and did not mention this to anyone for several weeks.

Now imagine that instead of placing it in t inet, I had opened up the black box and called out to Mack's ashes, ' , come out!" In my grief and desperation, I can't say the thought w 't have crossed my mind. But this would have been crazy. Life does ne from death. Death is final. That's what makes it so difficult. Ne ain will Mack sit with us at the table. We will never laugh together, worship together, and he will never see his brothers marry or meet his nephews and nieces. No more bonfires. No more Christmases. No more hugs. All the rest of our lives we must live without Mack. This never-ness is so very painful.

But when Jesus yelled into the grave, there was a rustling sound that came from inside the tomb. The crowd stood there looking at the hole, and moments later a figure appeared. The dead man came out, his hands and feet wrapped with strips of linen, and a cloth around his face. As everyone squealed and screamed and just stood there with their mouths wide open, Jesus said to them, "Take off the grave clothes and let him go."

So Lazarus, as dead as a worm that was unable to escape a hot summer sidewalk, was standing there completely alive. All of his organs were working again. His heart started beating again for the first time in four days. He stood there with functioning organs and no brain damage. If this is hard to believe, good. That means you're paying attention. Jesus brought life from death, and that's a miracle.

How can the impossible be possible?

Remember I told you that when Martha first heard that Jesus was finally coming to Bethany, she went out to meet him, and she and Jesus had a really interesting conversation? Let's go back to that conversation now:

> "Lord," Martha said to Jesus, "if you had been here, my brother would not have died. But I know that even now God will give you whatever you ask."
>
> Jesus said to her, "Your brother will rise again."
>
> Martha answered, "I know he will rise again in the resurrection at the last day."
>
> Jesus said to her, "I am the resurrection and the life. The one who believes in me will live, even though they die; and whoever lives by believing in me will never die. Do you believe this?"

When Jesus told Martha Lazarus would rise again, she thought He was talking about life after death—how Lazarus would have eternal life in Heaven. And Jesus affirms Martha's comment. When someone believes in Jesus, their spirit will never die even when they die physically. But Jesus said something else here that is significant. We already knew that Jesus claimed to bring us life to the full. But now Jesus is saying, "I AM the Life. I AM the resurrection." Life to the full isn't just something Jesus hands out--it is actually found in Himself.

Jesus says *He is* the life, and He can conquer spiritual death. And then to prove it, He goes into town and demonstrates He has power over death by conquering Lazarus' physical death. It's as if The Life is saying, "Spiritual death? No problem. I can conquer that. Physical death? No problem. I can conquer that too. Watch!"

The loss of my son has been devastating. But I take great comfort in knowing that Jesus is the resurrection and the life. Mack believed in Jesus. Because Mack lived by believing in Jesus, I know that he is with Jesus in heaven today, even though his earthly body is no longer alive. Death was not the end of Lazarus' story, and it is not the end of Mack's, either.

After claiming to be the Resurrection and the Life, Jesus asked Martha a powerful question, "Do you believe this?" Martha affirmed she did and was delighted to see Jesus back up His claim a few minutes later. But not everyone believed. In fact, even after Jesus performed this miracle, some of the eye witnesses went to the religious leaders (called Pharisees) to tell them what Jesus had done. They had already had their eye on Jesus. He wasn't educated in their religious schools, he didn't have their religious credentials, he didn't hold to their religious rules though He was Jewish, and most alarmingly He claimed to be the Life—something only God could claim.

So when they learned that this loose cannon, Jesus, now had power to raise the dead, they called a special Sanhedrin (the ruling council) meeting to discuss their options. "What are we going to do?" they asked. "Here is this man performing many signs. If we let him go on like this, everyone will believe in him, and then the Romans will come and take away both our temple and our nation."

Then one of them, named Caiaphas, who was high priest that year, spoke up, "You know nothing at all! You do not realize that it is better for you that one man die for the people than that the whole nation perish."

People have always been divided about Jesus. Some rejected Jesus and began to plot ways to kill him. While others, like Martha, believed that He was the Life, as He claimed to be. What if I were to ask you the same question Jesus asked Martha: "I am the resurrection and the life. The one who believes in me will live, even though they die; and whoever lives by believing in me will never die. Do you believe this?"[18]

Do you believe Jesus' claim to be the Life?

If you are not sure you do, that's okay. Don't panic. It's a lot to take in. But please don't stop reading now.

---

[18] John 11:25

10

NOT DOUG'S BIGGEST ISSUE

Pete and I met when we were three years old. As we grew up, we enjoyed going on adventures together. Well, Pete loved adventures. I think I mostly loved the *idea* of adventures. We were especially excited about any opportunity to experience the great outdoors--hiking, caving, climbing, exploring and canoeing down rivers. The summer before our sophomore year of high school, Pete had acquired a topographic map of Rock Bridge State Park, a 2,273-acre geological preserve just south of our home town of Columbia, Missouri. According to our calculations, there appeared to be a waterfall feature deep in the wilderness, a few miles up a riverbed.

The blazingly hot and humid August afternoon was not ideal for hiking. But we had become busy high school kids with work, sports and Pete's marching band schedule, so we opted to seize the day.

After a few hours of hiking along wobbly river bed rocks, we had only ventured a couple of miles. We pulled out Pete's map and guessed we were only half the distance to the waterfall. And because it was the dry season, it wasn't even an actual waterfall anyway. Pete had a trombone lesson at 6:30 pm so we discussed our options. Should we continue or turn around and head back home?

We noticed a cliff off to our right. Leading up to that cliff was a boulder field. So we made the decision to stop hiking, boulder up to the base of the cliff, then climb the cliff to see what was on top.

We did not have any harnesses, climbing ropes, helmets, belay devices, bolts, or anything to catch a fall. People call this type of climbing "free soloing." It is nice because there is no set up, hassle, or ropes. The risk is,

of course, that *there are no ropes!* If you fall, ee fall until you hit the
rocks at the bottom of the cliff which resu serious injury or worse.

If an adult with a fully developed prefront: ex (the self-monitoring,
problem-solving and decision-making part e brain) had been with us,
he would have certainly pointed out the ris our impulsive plan and
helped us make a more informed decision. t was just the two of us
high school boys, so we navigated the bou eld, reached the bottom of
the cliff and began to climb. This cliff, like cliffs in Missouri, was
made of gray and flaky limestone deposits. ingly secure rock chunks
were deceptively detached from the wall a ld easily break off when
you put weight on them. So Pete and I hac uple of rules when climbing.
First, we always needed three points of co so we could move only one
foot or one hand at a time. Second, we wo iple check every rock before
putting weight on it. We hoped these rules d keep us safe while free
soloing.

I was about twenty feet up and Pete was tc ight, about twenty-five feet
up. Things were going well when suddenly of my peripheral vision, I
saw Pete begin to fall. I watched him fall b nd down, twisting and
turning. He seemed to fall for a long time, hen he landed awkwardly
on boulders in a belly flop with a thud—h and hands first, and then
his legs, one leg in front of the other.

I don't recall climbing down the cliff and r g to his side. My mind was
a blur. The next thing I remember, I founc elf at Pete's side, looking at
his broken and bruised body. I didn't knov had a back injury, but I
could see that he was still alive. In that mo I had one goal, one focus,
one job in the world: I needed to get my l iend the help that he so
desperately needed. This is what friends dc ndship is taking care of
each other when their heart or body is bro True friendship is always
being there for a friend when they fall. Pet in serious trouble, and all
that mattered was my best friend.[19]

[19] Eventually we made it out of the forest and ved through the experience
and he was not paralyzed. He did, however, ha ry long and painful road to
recovery. He is happily married with grown kic is own, and still occasionally
breaks bones on his adventures. But neither Pe I have solo-climbed since

I'm not unique. This is what true friends have always done for one another. In fact, a few thousand years ago there was a man who was paralyzed. I don't know his name, so I will call him Doug. Doug's friends had heard of Jesus the miracle worker. Even without advertisements, social media or a public relations campaign, word about Jesus had spread far and wide. Nobody said the kind of things Jesus said, and no one did the kind of things Jesus did. If the rumors were true, if Jesus really brought sight to the blind, healed a withered hand, and brought a man back to life, these guys were committed to doing whatever it took to get Doug in front of Him!

Two thousand years ago in the Middle East, most people with disabilities had extremely limited career choices. More times than not, they became beggars. Doug's disability kept him from running and playing and dancing. It would likely keep him from getting a job, he might not get married and have kids, and he would never get to do many of the wonderful things able-bodied people get to do. If Doug's friends could just get him in front of Jesus, perhaps he would receive a miracle from the one who claimed to be Life.

They placed Doug onto a stretcher and carried him to where Jesus was teaching. But when they arrived they found that the house was already packed with people from all the surrounding towns. Jesus was even more famous than they anticipated. Many people were curious and many were seeking healing. The Pharisees and teachers of the law were there as well. They were deeply concerned about Jesus' teaching, and now that He was performing miracles, they were looking for evidence to eliminate Him.

As Doug's friends stood outside the house holding his stretcher, they discussed their options. They could wait until after Jesus' speech and try to catch Him on the way out of the house, but this was risky. There were people everywhere, and many of them looked like they also hoped to get Jesus' attention as he left the house. They could come back a different day, but Jesus' itinerary was unpublished and unpredictable. They could push Doug's limp body through an open window onto some Pharisees' heads, but that would just be awkward. There were no good options. The most

---

because, now that our prefrontal cortexes are fully developed, we realize it is a terribly stupid thing to do.

logical thing would be to turn back around. They were already exhausted from carrying him. They had been good friends and had made a valiant effort.

"Wait. What if we carried Doug up on the roof?" one of the friends proposed. Roofs in Jesus' day were constructed of tree poles which were spaced about 2-3 feet apart. Next small branches and palm fronds were laid on top and covered with a layer of leaves and dirt. The top layer was clay that was rolled flat with stone rollers. "What if we determined where Jesus was standing in the house, and then we removed a section of the roof large enough to lower Doug down in front of Him?" It was a wild idea; outlandish, desperate and mildly destructive.

This was a terrible idea for many reasons. Would the homeowner charge them with vandalism? What would the religious leaders think about the destruction of property? Whose house was this anyway? Furthermore, none of them knew how Jesus would react. There was no guarantee He would heal Doug. They would definitely be interrupting His speech to all those serious and important religious people. There was a chance this plan would do nothing more than make Jesus, the homeowner, and the religious leaders angry.

Perhaps their prefrontal cortexes weren't fully developed and that's why they proposed such a preposterous plan. Or, more likely, the hope that Doug might actually be healed outweighed all the risks, so they decided to go for it. After much effort, they got Doug on the roof, created a hole and lowered him down until he was awkwardly suspended right in the middle of the crowd, just floating there in front of Jesus. Jesus stopped speaking. He looked into Doug's eyes, then He looked up at the four friends. And when Jesus saw their faith, he said to Doug, "Friend, your sins are forgiven."

I can imagine the friends on the roof, holding tightly onto the ropes. "What did He say?"

"He said, 'Friend, your sins are forgiven.'"

What a bizarre thing for Jesus to say! These friends clearly hadn't carried Doug on a mat all that way and lowered him in through a hole in the roof of a house because Doug was a sinner!

Doug was a person, and as a member of the human race he had naturally inherited a sinful nature just like everybody else. Long ago Adam and Eve sinned by disobeying God in the Garden of Eden, and sin entered into the world. They had children who also inherited the sin-nature, and they had sinful children, and so on. As a result, Doug sometimes exhibited all the ugly qualities that separate humans from a perfect, holy God.

The Pharisees and the teachers of the law were also taken aback by Jesus' words: "Friend, your sins are forgiven." They began thinking to themselves, "Who is this fellow who speaks blasphemy? Who can forgive sins but God alone?"

Theologically-speaking, the religious leaders were correct: only God can forgive sins. They knew that Jesus wasn't personally forgiving Doug. It wasn't like Doug had been mean to Jesus the previous week, and now Jesus was saying, "Hey Doug, remember last week? No sweat man, I forgive you." No, Jesus was speaking to Doug on behalf of God. He was forgiving Doug's sin debt entirely.

This is why the Pharisees called this blasphemy. Blasphemy is when one claims to be God, or does or says something that only God should do or say. The Pharisees were correct: If Jesus was not in fact Deity as He claimed, His words would be blasphemous. But what if Jesus was, in fact, God in the flesh?

Jesus knew exactly what the religious guys were thinking so he asked, "Why are you thinking these things in your hearts? Which is easier: to say, 'Your sins are forgiven,' or to say, 'Get up and walk'? But I want you to know that the Son of Man has authority on earth to forgive sins." So he said to the paralyzed man, "I tell you, get up, take your mat and go home." Immediately Doug stood up in front of them, picked up his mat and went home praising God. Everyone was amazed and gave praise to God. They were filled with awe and said, "We have seen remarkable things today!"[20]

Jesus performed two miracles that day. The smaller one was to heal Doug, who entered the room on a mat lowered through the roof by some friends

---

[20] Luke 5:23-26

and was miraculously able to walk out on his own two legs, carrying the mat. Doug and his friends thought his disability was his greatest need. But Jesus highlighted Doug's greatest need in His first miracle: Doug's need to be forgiven for his sin. Sin is also my biggest issue. It was Mack's. And it's yours as well.

Maybe, like Doug, you have a disability. It might be physical, emotional, social or intellectual--or a combination of several. Maybe you look at yourself as too ugly, dumb, unathletic, unpopular, or insecure. It is natural to assume that one (or more) of these is your greatest issue. But it is nothing compared to your spiritual disability--your sin-nature, because it is actually killing you. Sin always leads to death.

The Bible tells us that sin leads to death in three ways:

1. Spiritual death: You have likely noticed the darkness, the brokenness, and the separation you know exists between yourself and God. No matter how good you try to be, you have the nagging feeling it's just not good enough. That's spiritual death. Your sin has cut you off from Jesus, the Life.

2. Physical death: When your brain stops functioning and your heart stops beating and your physical body begins to decay, this is physical death. And God says it is a result of sin.

3. Eternal death: When you combine death #1 and death #2, you get death #3. That is, when you are spiritually dead, separated from God, and your physical body dies, your spirit continues in that state of separation from God for all eternity. This is called Hell.

I have sinned and deserve death and so have you[21]. Everyone is in the same dead-end scenario.[22]

Let's say I think you are super cool. I can't stand the idea of you dying spiritually for your sins, so I decide to make the ultimate sacrifice—I will die to pay your sin debt for you so you don't have to. Can I do that? No, I have my own sin debt to pay. I can't die twice. What if you think I'm amazing and worth dying for, so you agree to pay my sin debt? That would

---

[21] Romans 6:23

[22] Romans 3:23

be incredibly kind of you, but can you actually do that? No, you have your own death to die. The only way anyone could die for another person's sins is if that person lived a perfect and holy life.

This is tough news. We are all victims. People have sinned and hurt us. But we are all villains who have hurt other people too. We have all separated ourselves from our perfect Creator. And we all deserve death three ways: spiritual, physical and eternal.

Somebody asked me recently why a good God would send people to Hell. I appreciate the question, but it's the wrong question because God doesn't send anyone to Hell. Rather, we are already headed toward Hell, all on our own. Remember sin and death weren't in God's original plan. We brought death into our world when we chose sin over God.

Jesus knew Doug's biggest need was to be forgiven of his deadly sin condition. And Jesus knows your greatest need is to be forgiven from the sin that is currently physically and spiritually killing you.

God hates *sin*! He doesn't hate *you*. Why does He hate sin? *Because He loves you.*

When Mack was barely old enough to walk, a big dog got loose in our neighborhood and jumped onto him, slamming him down onto the pavement. It all happened so fast. The dog was on my toddler's chest and terrified little Mackie began to scream in terror. I didn't know this dog. I didn't know if he was going to maul my baby boy's beautiful face or just lick him, but in that split moment, I hated that dog! I hated the dog *because* I loved my son. The dog was a potential threat to my toddler's life, so I threw the dog off of Mack and swept my son up into my arms. God is crazy about you, and the sin-nature is threatening your life. He created you to experience life to the full, and nothing will destroy you more

than sin.

Perhaps Doug left the house that day mor ted about being able to walk than having his sins forgiven. But I'm fairl ain that he had no idea how much those words, "Friend, your sins are en" would cost Jesus in the not too distant future.

11

HOW WE RUINED EVERYTHING

A while ago, there was no space or distance between anything, because there was nothing. There was no time. No matter. No molecules. No light. No cells. No life. And nothing with which to make anything else. There was just nothing. Nothing at all. And then God spoke.

This is what we carbon-based lifeforms who exist in space-time refer to as The Beginning. This is the moment when God, who had no beginning, spoke the Universe we live in into existence. The Bible doesn't give us much information about how God did this. But as the Creator, He was able to speak everything out of nothing. He just said, "Let there be light," and there was light.[23]

God created planets, black holes, and trillions of galaxy clusters. In one particular galaxy He spoke a little blue planet into existence. He made Earth just the right size. If He had made it too big, gravity would have been too strong for anything to survive. Everything would just be stuck to the planet, too heavy to move. If He made the Earth too small, everything would just float away. God also set the Earth to revolve the perfect distance away from just the right type and size of star. God set Earth up to receive the absolute perfect amount of heat and light to allow life to be created and support it. Any tiny miscalculation in any of the million variables in the design and creation of our planet would have made the Earth uninhabitable, but God placed it just the perfect spot in the cosmos.

God designed an atmosphere to moderate the temperature and protect His creation from ultraviolet radiation. He created oxygen, water and gravity.

---

[23] Genesis 1:3

He created a cycle in which plants help animals breathe by producing oxygen, and animals help plants by providing them with carbon dioxide. He went on and on like this, designing an intricate, fascinating, complex and stunningly beautiful world. Then He stepped back to look at all that He had made, and saw that it was very good.[24]

It was beautiful, harmonious, and plentiful. There was no pollution, war, disease, crime, sickness, hunger, disaster, or death. It was good.

An Italian guy by the name of Michelangelo di Lodovico Buonarroti Simoni (or Michelangelo for short, or Mic for very short) painted the ceiling in the Sistine Chapel in the Vatican palace. I'm sure you've heard of it. Many people say it is unsurpassed in scale and beauty. It leaves visitors breathless, in awe of Michelangelo's incredible talent. In the same way, God created the Universe to demonstrate His glory. We actually get to live our lives *in* His 3-D masterpiece. When we look up at the stars, we see His great power and mighty strength.[25] When we look at all the creatures God has made, from microscopic bacteria to the Antarctic blue whale, which can weigh up to 400,000 pounds (that's like 33 elephants) we see God's handiwork on display.[26] I marvel at God's creation every day. I see his handiwork in the puppy currently taking a nap next to me as I write this paragraph. Since the creation of the world God's invisible qualities, like His eternal power and divine nature, have been clearly seen.[27] Just by taking a moment to look around and soak in the masterpiece you are living in, you can begin to take in the magnificence of God. We, like everything else, were created to glorify God. It's our purpose.

Just like the toaster that was carefully designed and created to toast things, we have a purpose. A function. And that purpose is to bring glory to God. We have been designed specifically to enjoy life and intimacy with the God who created us.

But I suspect you've noticed that life is far from perfect. If you watch the news, you don't see stories of people living life to the full, enjoying intimacy

---

[24] Genesis 1:31
[25] Isaiah 40:26
[26] Psalm 104:24-25
[27] Romans 1:20

with God as they were designed to do. It's clear that the world is not experiencing the love, joy, peace, patience, kindness, goodness, faithfulness, gentleness, and self-control[28] that flows from a connection to the Creator. On the contrary, things are pretty messed up.

We see war, stress, pain, disaster, suicide, rioting, anger, famine, and human trafficking. We see so many ugly things coming out of the hearts of people: deeds of greed, wickedness, deceit, indecent behavior, envy, slander, pride, and foolishness[29] to name a few. Our world is polluted with chemicals, genetically modified food, loneliness, scammers and hackers. The Bible says that even natural disasters, like disease, hurricanes, earthquakes and deadly viral infections are a result of our rebellion against God. Our sin ruined everything.

This is hard to hear, but we need to deal with reality: our sin has disconnected us from the Source of Life, Jesus. We see it in the world around us, but we see it in ourselves as well. It's why you may feel dead inside. It's why you do things you hate. It's why you hurt, and why you hurt others.

Mack was born to sinners and inherited our sinful, separated condition. Once, when he was a tiny one-year-old, Amy was holding him while talking to some friends. Out of nowhere, Mack turned and slapped his mother—hard—right in the face for no apparent reason at all. Amy was surprised and Mack was embarrassed. He knew, even as a baby, that slapping one's mother is not the right thing to do. He immediately looked down and began to wiggle his fingers. It was actually pretty hilarious, but we tried not to laugh because this wasn't a habit we wanted to reinforce. If you don't think humans have inherited the sin nature, spend an hour in childcare and watch the way toddlers treat each other. The fights over a

[28] Galatians 5:22-23
[29] Mark 7:22 NASB

certain toy, despite the fact that the toy-to-kid ratio is 30-to-1, can get heated very quickly.

It all started with Adam and Eve in the Garden of Eden, when humans first rebelled against God. Sin came into the world through Adam, and death through sin, and so death spread to all of us because everyone has sinned.[30] Every descendant of Adam and Eve (including us) have inherited and endorsed their rebellion and we all have earned physical, spiritual and eternal death. Some people will tell you that sinning is fun, it won't kill you. Some even celebrate their sin—they're proud of it. But God is clear that "neither the sexually immoral nor idolaters nor adulterers nor men who have sex with men nor thieves nor the greedy nor drunkards nor slanderers nor swindlers will inherit the kingdom of God."[31]

No one wants to die, so we try to find life on our own. For instance, in junior high I thought popularity might bring me life so I saved up enough money to buy some Levi® 501 jeans with the little red tag on the back pocket. These were the cool jeans that all the cool kids were wearing so I thought this might be my ticket to living life to the full. But my plan backfired. No one noticed what jeans I was wearing. If they had noticed I was wearing Levi's, I wouldn't have suddenly become popular. And even if my Levi's made me popular, popularity would have not brought me life to the full.

I tried to be the weird guy, and I got people to laugh at me, but this did not bring life. I learned to play the electric guitar and joined a rock band but people weren't impressed. I tried sports, but that plan didn't pan out at all. And even if I had been the world's best athlete, musician or comedian, I would have struggled until I discovered the truth: life to the full can only be found in Jesus.

You can make fun of me if you want. Of course Levi's jeans don't bring life to the full! But if you do a quick assessment of your life—you're likely doing the same thing, even if you are an adult. Is it money? Power? Entertainment? Sex? Possessions? Control? Influence? Busyness? Travel? How are you subconsciously trying to cover up the sin disease that makes

---

[30] Romans 5:12

[31] 1 Corinthians 6:9-10

you spiritually dead?

Jesus often used the term *eternal life* to describe this life to the full:

- Whoever hears Jesus' words and believes in God the Father will have *eternal life* and will not be judged but has crossed over from death to *life.*[32]
- God the Father's will is that everyone who looks to Jesus and believes in Him shall have *eternal life.*[33]
- Jesus said He is the *bread of life.* Unlike regular bread that you can eat and still die, Jesus is living bread from heaven. If anyone eats of this bread, they will live forever.[34]
- Whoever believes in Him has *eternal life,* but whoever rejects Him will not see life.[35]
- God loved the world so much that he gave his one and only Son, that whoever believes in Him shall not perish but have *eternal life.*[36]
- Jesus said, "I am the way and the truth and the *life.* No one comes to the Father except through Me."[37]

Remember that in the beginning, Jesus made literally everything. In Jesus was life, and that life was the light of all mankind.[38] Then humans introduced sin and death.

So 2,000 years ago Jesus became human to visit the Earth He created, in person. And He was pretty doggone clear about who He is and what He can do and why He came. He said it many times, to many people, in many different ways: Jesus is life. He is eternal life. He is the only life. There's no other place to find life. He is the way to have eternal life. Come to Him if you want to cross over from death to life.

We are physically dying, spiritually dead and in desperate need of what Jesus alone can offer: life. So how do we receive what Jesus offers?

---

[32] John 5:24
[33] John 6:40
[34] John 6:48
[35] John 3:36
[36] John 3:16
[37] John 14:6
[38] John 1:4

12

OH, BUT I KNOW WHAT IT'S LIKE

When Jesus healed the guy we named "Doug," the religious leaders were furious. Not because of the hole Doug's friends had made in the roof, and not because Doug could walk, but because Jesus had forgiven Doug's sins. They had already concluded that Jesus couldn't be God, so from their perspective every God-like thing Jesus did was blasphemy. Even the astonishing miracle Jesus performed right in front of their faces didn't change their minds. Instead, they were angry.

Jesus had many interactions like this with the religious elite. While many people saw Him for who He was and put their faith in him, the self-righteous priests became more and more irritated. One wintery day in Jerusalem they gathered around him at a festival. "If you are the Messiah, tell us plainly," they demanded.

Jesus answered, "I did tell you, but you do not believe. The works I do in my Father's name testify about me, but you do not believe because you are not my sheep. My sheep listen to my voice; I know them, and they follow me. I give them eternal life, and they shall never perish; no one will snatch them out of my hand. My Father, who has given them to me, is greater than all; no one can snatch them out of my Father's hand. I and the Father are one."

They heard His answer loud and clear, so they picked up stones to stone him. Today, if someone walks around claiming to be God, people either feel sorry for him, make fun of him, or try to get him psychiatric help. But in Jesus' day, the blasphemer was thrown into a pit and they threw rocks at him until he was dead. That is a shockingly brutal way to handle blasphemy. As you can imagine, not many walked around claiming to be one with God.

Jesus saw that they had picked up stones to throw at Him, so He asked, "I have shown you many good works from the Father. For which of these do you stone me?"

"We are not stoning you for any good work," they replied, "but for blasphemy, because you, a mere man, claim to be God."[39]

I've met people who think of Jesus as a great moral teacher, but they are not sure if Jesus was actually God. I totally understand how the idea of God dwelling in a human body is a wild concept. But Jesus couldn't be a great moral teacher if His teaching was centered on a big lie about His identity.

If Jesus wasn't God, but repeatedly claimed to be, then either He was a liar who fooled millions of people or he had a very serious mental illness and so He legitimately thought He was God. There are people who have a mental illness called delusional disorder, in which a person cannot tell what is real from what is imagined. The problem with these two theories, of course, is the blatantly obvious fact that Jesus was the most attractive person who ever lived. The worldwide following and impact of Jesus' life provides overwhelming evidence that Jesus lived a life worth imitating in every way.

The most rational conclusion is that Jesus became human and made His dwelling among us.[40] Jesus was actually who He said He was: the Way, the Truth, and the Life. All the evidence we have about Jesus proves He was the most truthful, sane, logical, brilliant, balanced, intelligent, thoughtful, loving, grace-filled and non-crazy person who ever lived.

Jesus slipped out of that precarious near-death situation, but the religious leaders had heard and seen enough. They would no longer allow some random guy to walk around claiming to be God, and inexplicably prove it by walking on water, bringing the dead back to life, feeding 5,000 people from five loaves of bread and two fish, and healing the blind, the deaf, and a guy we are calling Doug.[41] Soon thousands of people were following Jesus and they were losing more and more control every day. They felt it was

---

[39] John 10:22-33

[40] John 1:14

[41] Still not his real name.

their duty to preserve the religious structure of society, and, if they didn't stop Jesus' blasphemy, who would?

So they made a plan. We can read in Mark 14 how they conspired with Judas, one of Jesus' disciples, and had Jesus arrested at night. He was brought before their religious counsel (called the "Sanhedrin") in a late night trial. They were looking for evidence against Jesus so that they could put him to death. Eventually, the high priest stood up and asked Jesus, "Are you the Messiah, the Son of the Blessed One?"

"I am," said Jesus. "And you will see the Son of Man sitting at the right hand of the Mighty One and coming on the clouds of heaven."

The high priest tore his clothes. "Why do we need any more witnesses?" he asked. "You have heard the blasphemy. What do you think?"

They all condemned Jesus as worthy of death. Then some began to spit at him; they blindfolded him, struck him with their fists, and said, "Prophesy!" And the guards took him and beat him.[42]

You can read the horrific account for yourself in the Bible: Jesus' body was absolutely brutalized behind comprehension. He was beaten, spit on, mocked, forced to wear a crown of thorns, whipped within an inch of His life, and eventually nailed to a cross where He suffocated to death.

It makes me nauseous to think of anyone being tortured to death in this indescribably gruesome and disgusting way. It breaks my heart, but I do not feel sorry for Jesus. I think a lot of people think of Jesus as a hippie guy who was kind of a homeless spiritual guru in sandals. He walked around randomly talking about love and peace and told everyone to play nice. But make no mistake: Jesus was a Man on a mission. And His mission was to die.

As the world's only perfect Person, He was the only one who had not earned the death penalty. So, when He died, He was not dying for His sins. He was dying for Mack's sins, for my sins, and for your sins. Jesus got what

---

[42] Mark 14:55-65

we deserved.

When Jesus claimed to be the Messiah, He knew exactly what would happen next. And when Jesus told Doug that His sins were forgiven, they were more than just empty words spoken to irritate the religious leaders standing by. On the cross, Jesus paid Doug's death penalty. And He paid mine. And He paid yours.

The night Mack died, I can't even begin to describe the emotions and pain and confusion that were swirling around in my brain. My whole world was a nightmare. I couldn't even wrap my mind around the utter horror of the news that Mack's body was lifeless and his spirit had departed. Among the many heavy and confusing emotions was a profound sense of loneliness. I didn't know anyone else who had lost a son. No one could possibly understand what I was feeling. I was completely, totally undone.

As I laid there in bed, thinking that no one could relate to my pain, I heard the Lord whisper to my spirit, *"Oh friend, but I know what it's like."* I can't describe it, but suddenly I felt an overwhelming sense of comfort and peace. I was not alone—even in the darkest valley of the shadow of death. My pain and grief did not diminish, but I was no longer alone, because God the Father reminded me that He also knows the pain of losing a son to death. This may sound crazy, but in the worst-case scenario nightmare I was living, I felt a unique connection with the heart of God the Father. Knowing that God is an ever-present help in trouble has carried me more than I could ever begin to explain.

So here is the million-dollar question that has baffled people for two thousand years: *Why?*

Why would God love you and me like this? Why would God's plan be for His sinless, perfect Son to be brutally murdered for our sins?

If I were God, I would have considered a much more simple and logical way to treat the little lifeforms on one of my trillions of planets that had rebelled against me. I could just flick my pinkie finger and they would cease to exist. But God's perfect plan wasn't destruction, it was love.

There is no good answer to this question. We did absolutely nothing to deserve His love. We didn't earn it. God doesn't owe us anything. Our good deeds couldn't possibly impress Him enough to make Jesus' torture and brutal sacrifice worthwhile. That's why Christians sing *Amazing* Grace—because His grace is *amazing*!

The reality is that God loves you because He made you, you are His, and He believes you are worth dying for. It is by God's grace that we have the opportunity to cross over from death to life. Our good works have nothing to do with it. Eternal life is a gift, purchased at a high price by Jesus on the cross, and given freely to us.[43]

---

[43] Ephesians 2:8-9

13

THE MOST EPIC EVENT IN HUMAN HISTORY

The news of Mack's sudden death rocked me to my core. I remember a coworker calling a few weeks after he died to ask how I was doing. "Well," I said, "I got up and took a shower this morning." He laughed, thinking that I was joking. "No, I'm serious. For me, today, that was a win."

Events like these are like earthquakes. One moment everything is fine, and the next moment your whole world is reduced to rubble. When the doctor says you have cancer; when your home burns to the ground; when the accident leaves you paralyzed; when you are victimized and assaulted by someone you trusted; when death steals someone you love. An earthquake comes out of nowhere, your world is completely rocked and you have no idea where to turn.

The disciples had been with Jesus for three years. They traveled with him, watched Him perform miracles, listened as He taught people about the Kingdom of God, and marveled at how He authentically loved the people everyone else had cast aside. He was their leader, their hope, their Savior, their friend, their teacher, and their future. And suddenly, Jesus had been violently brutalized and tortured to death. Jesus' death on the cross came with an earthquake, not only figuratively but literally[44] as well.

One of Jesus' followers took Jesus' dead body, wrapped it in a clean linen cloth, placed it in his own tomb that had been cut out of the rock, and a huge stone was rolled in front of the entrance.[45] The spear-stabbed, nail and thorn-pierced, whipped and beaten, lifeless shell that had contained the person of Jesus was laid in a cold, dark tomb. And there the corpse decomposed for three days.

---

[44] Matthew 27:51-52

[45] Matthew 27:57-60

Then three days later, Jesus, who claimed to be the Resurrection and the Life and had proven it by raising Lazarus and others from the dead, decided that it was time to not be dead any more. On the third day, Jesus conquered His own death!

Obviously this is impossible. How could a dead man make a decision to do anything unless this person was stronger than death itself? Yet Jesus' spirit returned to His physical body. His heart began beating and His organs started back up again. His wounds were miraculously healed and His brain function resumed. This was so shocking that many of the disciples had trouble believing it could be true.

Not too long ago we had friends over for dinner. We were still sitting at the table after the meal, and I glanced out the window where the kids were playing on the driveway. I saw my youngest son, Spencer, skateboarding while wearing his friend's baseball cap. I don't recall ever seeing him do this, but Mack skateboarded with a ball cap all the time. Just for a moment, I thought I saw Mack skateboarding on our driveway. A millisecond later my terrible reality came crashing back in on me and, without warning, my eyes welled up with tears.

But this isn't at all what happened with the disciples. This wasn't one disciple nudging another saying, "Whoa, dude, that hippie over there looks just like Jesus!" In fact, it *was* the resurrected Jesus, and he continued His ministry for another forty days.[46] The Bible records ten appearances, each showing a variety of where, when and to whom He spoke. Sometimes it was just to a few of His disciples, another time He spoke to a crowd of five hundred people. He continued His message about the Kingdom of God. Jesus really was the Resurrection and the Life, and He wanted everyone to know He was not just kidding around.

---

[46] Acts 1:3

I used to think of Jesus' resurrection as just another one of His miracles. Jesus walked on water, turned water into wine, and commanded a storm to stop. He healed people and pulled a coin from the mouth of a fish to pay some taxes. And, oh yeah, He also came back to life.

But now I understand Jesus' resurrection to be in a category all by itself, because if Jesus had done all those other miracles, been crucified and stayed dead like every other human in history, Life would not have conquered death. Death would have been stronger than all of us, even Jesus.

In the Bible, the Apostle Paul soundly rested his whole case for the Gospel on this one historical event: "If Christ has not been raised," he said, "our preaching is useless and so is your faith."[47] If Jesus didn't conquer death, the account of Jesus is just a cute little story with characters like Santa Claus, the Easter Bunny, Spiderman, or Luke Skywalker.

There are only two options: either Jesus actually rose from the dead or He did not. If He did, it was the most epic event in all of history. If the resurrection actually happened, we know that God exists and Jesus is His Son. If Jesus rose from the dead, then His words and teaching aren't pithy sayings, but the very words of God. We can know confidently that God loves us, we have infinite value, and the whole universe takes on meaning and purpose.

On the other hand, if Jesus stayed dead, then His death paid the price for His own sins, not ours. It means billions of Christians are deluded fools. Three hundred forty million Christians worldwide have needlessly suffered discrimination, unequal treatment and violent persecution. In 2020 alone, 4,761 people were killed because of their Christian faith, 4,277 Christians were arrested without legal proceedings or sentenced while already in prison, and 4,488 Christian places of worship were attacked.[48] All of this pain and suffering for no good reason. If Jesus was not the Life as He claimed, worship is pointless, missionaries have given their lives for no cause, and you've wasted your time reading this book.

---

[47] 1 Corinthians 15:14

[48] World Watch List 2020, Open Doors USA, Santa Ana, CA, http://OpenDoorsUSA.org/WWL

We buried Mack's ashes in a graveyard near Swope Park in Kansas City. We go visit the grave site every once in a while to cry, lament, and remember him. I don't really know what to do while I'm there. I just stand there with my hands in my pockets and give myself permission to cry. I stare at his name and the "1996 – 2020" on his gravestone, wishing he was still here. For Christmas, we decorated a little Christmas tree and put it on his grave. For his birthday, we painted rocks with happy birthday messages and left them there. For his death anniversary, we wrote messages to him on a potted plant. It feels weird to do these things. But it also feels weird not to.

Jim Morrison, the lead singer of the Doors, died of a heroin overdose in 1971. I have no idea why, but an estimated three million people still visit his grave each year in Paris. Six hundred thousand visit Elvis' grave each year. Michael Jackson's grave is in a private section of a cemetery, and even so thousands come each day to leave flowers just outside the gate.

Even though Jesus is the most famous, history-altering person to ever live, no one ever visits His grave because He doesn't have one. Jesus rose from the dead. He just borrowed a friend's tomb for the weekend and then gave it back. It was just a short-term loan.

The Life died, then the Life conquered death. If He can defeat His own death, He can defeat yours as well. And all the evidence points to the fact that Jesus got up and walked out of His own grave. This changes everything.

You see, when we visit Mack's grave, we are simply visiting a monument that has his name engraved into it. But Mack, our son—the sweet guy who laughed till he cried, had the twinkle in his eye, and possessed the gift of photography; the guy who made everyone feel special and valuable—*that* Mack isn't buried in the ground. The human remains of the body that Mack lived in for 24 years is there, but because Jesus conquered His own death,

He conquered death once and for all. He has conquered my eternal death, He conquered Mack's eternal death, and He wants to conquer yours as well.

Today, Mack is with Jesus. And in the end, this is all that matters.

14
THE PROPOSAL

Growing up, every Christmastime my parents and brother and I would stay at an apartment at Town Center Plaza in Kansas City to enjoy the Christmas lights, shop, eat out, and put together puzzles. In 1991 I brought my girlfriend along.

While Mom distracted Amy, I sneaked away to Colonial Presbyterian Church, where I had done an internship the previous summer. I put a ring in a little stocking by a window where I first told Amy I loved her, set up a jam box with a specially-made mix tape cued up just perfectly, and made other arrangements. I got back to the apartment for pizza with my family, then I suggested to Amy that we go for a drive, just the two of us. We somehow ended up at Colonial that evening, and for some inexplicable reason I happened to have a key to the church in my pocket. Amy was nervous we would get in trouble for sneaking around the church at night, but I suggested we go to our special window. And while Amy opened the stocking, I got down on one knee.

I had done all I could do at this point. I had executed my elaborate plan. I was literally kneeling before the girl I loved. She was holding my gift to her, the most expensive thing I had ever purchased, and my proposal had been submitted for her consideration: "Will you marry me?"

My question demanded a response. 'Yes' or 'No' are the two most obvious answers to my question. But one thing Amy could not do is ignore the question altogether. She couldn't pretend that I had not just offered to love and serve her in a life-long covenant relationship. My question was one which demanded an answer.[49]

In the same way, God has initiated an amazing, intricate, mind-boggling plan. Jesus came to Earth and lived a sinless life as a human being. He told us, over and over again, that He was the Life and yet people were divided. He endured suffering, shame and abuse and allowed us to murder Him. Why? Because you are His. He loves you that much. He would rather die so that you could have the opportunity to spend eternity with Him than watch you get what you earned from your sin: death.

Jesus has done all He could do at this point. He has executed His elaborate plan. He is holding out His gift to you, the most expensive thing anyone has ever purchased, and He has expressed His love to you. What is your response?

A lot of people think the response God wants is religion. Imagine that instead of saying, "Yes!" Amy put on a fancy purple robe with gold tassels, built an altar and began reciting poems about love. That would be super weird, right?

God is not impressed with fancy purple robes--our empty spiritual-looking activities. To God, this isn't a transaction in which He gives us eternal life and in return we go to church potlucks, give blood, and help with the parking team at our local megachurch. I'm not saying these aren't fine activities. I'm just saying that God doesn't want our religiously-motivated civic activities. He wants us to trust Him in an actual love relationship.

To help explain what trust looks like, let me go back to a day in the life of Jesus. In Luke 7, a religious Pharisee named Simon invited Jesus over for a meal. And a woman from the village showed up with a bottle of very expensive perfume. She didn't just look through the window at Jesus or stand awkwardly in the corner, but she came right up to Jesus while He was reclining at the table and she cried all over His feet. Then, letting down her hair, she dried His feet, kissed them, and anointed them with the perfume. If you're wondering if this was some sort of normal cultural activity that people used to do in Jesus' day, it wasn't. It's just as awkward and

---

[49] She said yes, by the way. And I think she really liked my mixtape.

inappropriate as it sounds.

Simon knew it was especially awkward because this wasn't any random lady kissing Jesus' feet. It was a woman who was known around town for being sexually active with a variety of people. Religious people wouldn't even associate with such a sinner. Simon thought to himself, "If this man was the prophet I thought he was, He would have known what kind of woman this is who is falling all over Him."

Jesus knew what Simon was thinking, so He told him this parable: "Two men were in debt to a banker. One owed five hundred silver pieces, the other fifty. Neither of them could pay up, and so the banker canceled both debts. Which of the two would be more grateful?"

Simon answered, "I suppose the one who was forgiven the most."

"That's right," said Jesus. Then turning to the woman, but speaking to Simon, he said, "Do you see this woman? I came to your home; you provided no water for my feet, but she rained tears on my feet and dried them with her hair. You gave me no greeting, but from the time I arrived she hasn't quit kissing my feet. You provided nothing for freshening up, but she has soothed my feet with perfume. Impressive, isn't it? She was forgiven many, many sins, and so she is very, very grateful. If the forgiveness is minimal, the gratitude is minimal."

Then Jesus spoke to her: "I forgive your sins."

That set the dinner guests talking behind his back: "Who does he think He is, forgiving sins!" (Again, Jesus doing something only God should be doing).

He ignored them and said to the woman, "Your faith has saved you. Go in peace."[50] And it's interesting, that last phrase Jesus uses: *your faith has saved you.*

Faith, in this instance, looks like being so in love with Jesus that you don't care how awkward it is or what people think. We don't know if this woman

---

[50] Luke 7:36-50

had been baptized, if she had prayed the "Sinner's Prayer," or if she had successfully passed her local church's new members' class. But she clearly was incredibly grateful and was not afraid to show it. And Jesus loved her faith.

Remember the story about the guy I called Doug, the guy whose friends let him down through the roof, right in front of Jesus? When Jesus saw Doug's friends' *faith*, He said to Doug, "Friend, your sins are forgiven."[51] Faith, in this instance, looked like making the extra effort—doing whatever it takes to get to Jesus. And Jesus loved their faith.

Another time a Roman army guy came up to Jesus and said, "Lord, my servant lies at home paralyzed, suffering terribly."

Jesus said to him, "Shall I come and heal him?"

The centurion replied, "Lord, I do not deserve to have you come under my roof. But just say the word, and my servant will be healed." When Jesus heard this, He was amazed and said to those following him, "Truly I tell you, I have not found anyone in Israel with such great faith." And He said to the centurion, "Go! Let it be done just as you believed it would." And his servant was healed at that moment. Faith, in this instance, looked like trusting Jesus at His word.

Scriptural accounts of what faith looks like may surprise you. It is never a religious activity that Jesus is excited about. It's never waving a thurible full of holy incense around or reciting a fancy prayer. Jesus gets excited when people actually trust Him. And He gave you life so that you may know Him. Sin killed that opportunity, so Jesus, the Life, died to give you the opportunity to re-establish that connection with Him.

There's a verse in the Bible that says, "For it is by grace you have been saved, through faith—and this is not from yourselves, it is the gift of God."[52] In other words, God did all the work. He loves you because you are His, not because of your performance. So what is an appropriate response to this great, abundant, abounding love?

---

[51] Luke 5:20

[52] Ephesians 2:8

We can either trust Jesus by faith, or excuse ourselves and walk away from Him.

If you've ever heard some ask why a good God would send people to Hell, the answer is, "He doesn't." Rather, He graciously has made a way for people to not go to Hell. He is the only One who could have saved us, and He did! Jesus offers an opportunity to have life in His kingdom—a place where love, worship, grace, goodness, joy and peace flow freely from His presence. There is another invitation this world offers—to choose one's self, own ideals and values over the authority of the Creator King. This choice is inherently destructive and leads to eternity apart from God.

Amy could have looked at the ring, looked at me, considered my proposal, and said, "Thanks, but no thanks." She could have walked away. You and I have that option too—to walk away from God's offer of a life-giving relationship with Himself. But before you do that, at least recognize that the God of the Universe is asking you to simply run to His arms—and trust Him with your life.

One day when Mack was just a few years old, he came running up to me crying. "Owie!" he said as he offered me his fat little foot. He sat down on my lap and sure enough, he had a little thorn in his foot. I got a pin and tweezers, and explained that I needed to poke at his foot with the needle to get the thorn out.

To get the healing he needed, Mack needed to trust me. He needed to surrender his foot to me, by faith.

Faith is more than acknowledging my existence. Mack couldn't just say, "Dad, I believe you exist." He needed to trust me.

Faith is more than mental assent. Mack co just say, "That's a good plan, Dad." He needed to trust me.

Faith occurred when Mack surrendered hi: so I could deal with the problem. Faith is when you surrender you: o that Jesus' death and resurrection can deal with your sin probler is is why life, acceptance, intimacy, love, joy, peace, purpose and yo identity can only be found through faith in Jesus. The Bible says that "Believe (trust, hope, have faith) in the Lord Jesus, you will be saved.'

[53] Acts 16:31

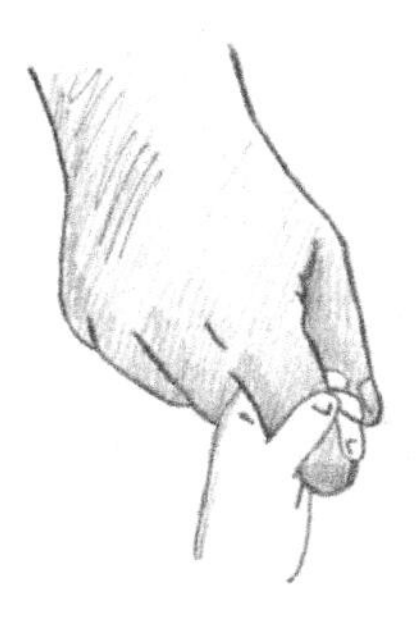

15

LIFE, FREEDOM, RELATIONSHIP AND ADOPTION

My family makes fun of me because I stop, kneel and pick up worms off the sidewalk after a rainstorm so I can throw them back in the grass. It just seems to me that frying to death on a hot summer sidewalk would be an awful way to die, even for a worm.

I love Kansas City barbecue, but I don't want to eat in restaurants that have paintings of pigs and cows on the wall. Call me crazy, but I don't want to think about who had to die so that I can enjoy my sandwich. Death makes my pulled pork less enjoyable.

I guess you could say I'm tender-hearted when it comes to death. If I care about worms and cattle, it stands to reason that ever since Mack died last year, I have felt a deep sadness. The feeling never completely goes away, and I don't think it ever will. When Mack died, a part of me died too. So I grieve because I am rich in love for him, but I can't express this love to him. So it remains lodged in my heart, unspent. It gathers up in my chest, sometimes around my eyes, and often expresses itself through a deep sigh. Grief is just love with no place to go.

But while I grieve, I also have joy because although Mack is not with me on Earth, he is very much alive. I have heard it said that if a person is only born once, they die twice. But if a person is born twice, they only die once. Mack was born twice—both physically and spiritually, so he is eternally alive with Christ. If Mack had been born only once, if he had refused God's gift of grace, he would have died twice—physically and eternally.

I am so thankful for Jesus' death on the cross; the Life died so that Mack might live. But we don't need to wait until we die physically to begin enjoying the gift of life that Jesus offers to us. When Jesus died for our sins, we were set free. He not only set us free from the death penalty, He set us free from prison!

But many of us act as though we're still chained to the sins that we committed while we were on death row. The Bible actually says it is for freedom that Christ has set us free![54] That seems like a Captain Obvious statement. (Why else would we be set free—if not to be free?) But we have a tendency to go back to our old ways, our old patterns, and our old destructive habits. Jesus died to forgive us of our sin, but He also died to set us free from sin!

He has set us free from fear, from destructive habits, from the same-old, same-old of always trying to get people to like us, and from the consequences of sin (like guilt, sexually transmitted diseases, incarceration, drug addictions, broken hearts, shattered relationships, feelings of worthlessness, pain, etc.).

The thief comes to steal and kill and destroy[55]. He tells us to watch this, think like this, drink this, indulge in this, smoke this, gratify sexual cravings, shoot this in your arm, let ugly and hurtful words fly from your mouth, and treat people as less than ourselves. But the more we indulge in these behaviors, the less satisfied we are. The feeling of emptiness pervades and prevails.

Jesus said He was the Truth, and He actually is the Truth. He never, ever lies to us. He was kind enough to give us His Word as a guide about how to

---

[54] Galatians 5:1

[55] John 10:10

live. His ways are always best. So if God, through His Word, tells us that things like "sexual immorality, impurity and debauchery; idolatry and witchcraft; hatred, discord, jealousy, fits of rage, selfish ambition, dissensions, factions and envy; drunkenness, and orgies"[56] are going to kill our souls, He is telling us the truth! There is no sin that brings life.

Sometimes people who are slaves to sin look at those who have freedom in Christ as the ones who are confined. Non-Christians can look at Christianity as a list of rules. And that can be true. Sometimes Christians experience one kind of freedom (from sin) and then walk right into another type of religious prison. But it's because we are free that we desire to honor God with our lives. We desire to obey Him not to impress Him, but because it is an overflow of deep gratitude in our hearts. His kindness leads us to repentance![57]

When Jesus died in our place, He not only gave us life and freedom, but a relationship with God Himself! "For God so loved the world that he gave His one and only Son, that whoever believes in Him shall not perish but have eternal life. For God did not send His Son into the world to condemn the world, but to save the world through Him. Whoever believes in Him is not condemned, but whoever does not believe stands condemned already because they have not believed in the name of God's one and only Son."[58]

God does not want to condemn us, He wants to be near us. He doesn't just love us—He actually enjoys us! The Creator King made us in His image, and He likes what He made, and now He wants to hang out! God created us so He could enjoy us, and so that we could enjoy Him. Jesus died to give us an actual, real, authentic relationship with God.

And beyond life, freedom and a relationship with Himself, Jesus died so that God could offer us adoption. "Yet to all who did receive him, to those who believed in his name, he gave the right to become children of God—children born not of natural descent, nor of human decision or a husband's will, but born of God."[59] Of course, we (like every person ever) have

---

[56] Galatians 5:19-21
[57] Romans 2:4
[58] John 3:16-17
[59] John 1:12-13

earthly parents. But most of us, even those of us who have been set free, still walk around like orphans. Many orphans live on the street. They don't know when, where or even if their next meal is coming. It is up to them to survive, to somehow do whatever it takes to survive. In the same way, we can live like orphans. We are driven to make money, get people's approval, have success, to somehow survive this thing we call "life." So we are stressed out, living in the streets, trying to fend for ourselves--while our Father who owns everything will gladly provide all we need.

"Just show up at my table!" the Lord invites us. "Listen, my child, if lame earthly parents know how to give good gifts to their children, how much more will I give good things to those who ask Me![60] I will supply all of your needs according to My riches in glory in Christ Jesus.[61] So do not be anxious, saying, 'What shall I eat?' or 'What shall I drink?' or 'What shall I wear?'[62] Just trust me. I am perfect. I love you perfectly. And I will never leave you or forsake you."[63]

While God the Father loves His children perfectly, it is not unusual for some of us to have baggage with the word "father." Our earthly parents can be distant, non-existent or even abusive. I get it. People are sinners. Some of these sinners are terrible at life, and some of them have kids. But God is the perfect parent you have always longed for. He will never abandon you, forget you, ignore you, desert you, mistreat you, or neglect you. God is perfect love.

If God is my Father, and God is your Father, that makes us siblings. If you ever wondered where you belong, now you know. In the family of God. You are no longer alone! You are a part of God's family—along with people of every nationality, ethnicity, and nation who also have responded to God's generous offer of life, freedom, relationship and adoption. "These are your brothers and sisters. Now you are no longer divided by ethnicity,

---

[60] Matthew 7:11

[61] Philippians 4:19

[62] Matthew 6:31-32

[63] Hebrews 13:5

occupation or gender—for all of you are one in Me."[64]

In Christ, we know our *identity*.

We know that we *matter* and our choices matter.

We know our *purpose*.

We know where we *belong*.

We know that we are created by Jesus and for a relationship with Jesus.

---

64 Galatians 3:28

16

ACT FOUR

Like any good American Dad, I passed my love of Star Wars on to Mack. I was eight years old when my Dad took me to see Star Wars in a theater in 1977, and my world was totally rocked. I was in awe of this epic story of spaceships, aliens, and lightsabers. The good guys, Luke, Han Solo and Chewbacca sneaked onto the Death Star to save Princess Leah from the bad guys, Darth Vader and his Stormtroopers. I collected the action figures, played Star Wars with my friends at recess (which consisted of running around saying, "Pew pew I got you!"), and I even traded in my Snoopy lunch box for a Star Wars one instead.

The Star Wars universe generated quite a bit of excitement, as well as confusion and controversy among the elementary kids in the seventies. For instance, how do lightsabers work? Do they chop off a person's hand (like, in the cantina) or make a person disappear completely (like, when Vader took a swing at Obi Wan)? Was his name Darth Vader or Dark Vader? If Stormtroopers fall down and die the moment they get shot, why did they wear armor?

The original Star Wars movie, like all good movies, has a grand story arc. As I see it, the story can be divided up into four acts. I'm going to list them below, so if you've been really busy since 1977 and haven't seen the original Star Wars movie yet, feel free to watch it before reading on.

Act One: There are aliens on other planets, many of them look just like people, and most of them speak English!

Act Two: All is not well. There is an evil Empire led by a big jerk in a giant helmet who is obsessed with controlling the galaxy. Darth (Dark?) Vader has a Death Star (it's no moon, it's a space station) with a gun big enough to blow up an entire planet.

Act Three: There is a plan. A small one-man fighter could drop a proton torpedo into a two meter wide thermal exhaust port on the Death Star. This port has a shaft that leads directly to the reactor system. A precise hit would start a chain reaction which should destroy the Death Star. So Luke and the other rebels attack the Death Star in their little X-Wing fighters. Sadly, many of the rebel pilots lose their lives in the battle.

Act Four: Against all odds Luke's torpedo blows up the Death Star and the movie ends with all of our heroes grinning, nodding and winking in an awkwardly silent celebratory assembly.

But what if Luke had missed the shot? The Empire would have blown up the Rebel base, all the good guys would be dead, and evil would have triumphed. The whole struggle would have felt pointless. Star Wars would have remained a B-movie and I certainly wouldn't have purchased a new lunch box.

Knowing the entire story arc from beginning to end helps us make sense of the struggle throughout the movie. Knowing that the Light Side beats the Dark Side somehow brings meaning to the struggle in the midst of the story.

If someone were to walk out during Act Three, they would not know the full story. They would have witnessed death and struggle, but would not have seen the victory in Act Four.

The Bible is God's historical record of the grand story arc of planet Earth. We may even refer to history as His story. (See what I did there?) The universe is not about me, and the people I come into contact with are not actors in *my* play. My life is not about me. No, you and I are a part of a grand story arc called reality.

The Bible, and the story arc we are living in, can be divided into four acts:

Act One: God creates everything. Human beings are made in God's image to have a love relationship with Himself. God is with people on Earth and everything is good.

Act Two: All is not well. People rebel against God, creating a rift. As a result, sin, pain, evil, suffering and death enter our story. Every person inherits a sinful nature and chooses to do that which God would have us not do.

Act Three: There is a plan. Though we are hopelessly lost and dead in our sins, and the only One who could help us is God Himself, He is kind and loving enough to do so. God sends His only Son to earth. Jesus dies on the cross to pay the price for our sins. This is the first part of God's plan to make everything right.

Act Four: Jesus returns to Earth, Satan is defeated, God's plan is complete and everything is made right. There is no more sin, pain, evil, suffering and death. Christ is victorious and everything is made new.

We are living in Act Three right now. As it turns out, our decision to give God the finger in Act Two was a terrible one, so now the horrific ramifications of separating ourselves from our Creator are unending. The struggle, sickness, pain, violence and death we experience in Act Three is gut-wrenching.

Mack's death was the result of his own and others' sin. He was betrayed and wounded, and his heart was deeply broken. In that sad, lost, disillusioned state, taking his own life felt to him like his only option. It wasn't his only option, but in his pain, he couldn't see clearly.

If we were living in a story arc with only three Acts, this would be the end. Everything sucks. Life is meaningless. The end. Roll credits.

Deep down, we all feel like we should live forever. Death feels wrong, like something is amiss. Yet we keep dying. Just as Mack suffered and died, so will I, and so will you. And if we think history only has three Acts, we are left wondering, why is God doing nothing to fix this problem? Either God is cruel, having the power to stop all of this suffering and choosing not to. Or He is weak, desiring to stop it but He is not able to.

Indeed, this is hard to wrestle through. God was with Mack when He died. He could have done something, He could have stopped it, and He had the power to step in. But He didn't.

I don't know why God allowed Mack to die on that date, at that time, in that way. I do not know the reason behind anyone's death, including mine or yours. I ask God "Why?" every day. And I'm not the only one. The Psalmist asks the same questions. "My God, my God, why have you forsaken me? Why are you so far off from saving me, so far from the cries of my anguish?"[65]

"Why, O Lord, do you stand far off? Why do you hide Yourself in times of trouble?"[66]

"Why must I go about mourning, oppressed by the enemy?"[67]

But when I step back to get a 10,000 foot view of the entire story arc as described in the Bible, I can know why Mack died. And I know why I will die, and why you will die. God gave us the option to fall into His open arms or reject Him, and I wish we hadn't used our free will to rebel against Him. The suffering and evil and pain we are enduring as a result of our defiance is awful. I wish we hadn't brought sin, death and destruction to our planet. But friends, please don't walk out of the theater, because there is an Act Four!

No one knows exactly when, but Jesus is coming back.[68] God has not given up on us.

Revelation gives us a glimpse of what our future with God will look like: "And I heard a loud voice from the throne saying, 'Look! God's dwelling

---

[65] Psalm 22:1

[66] Psalm 10:1

[67] Psalm 42:9

[68] Matthew 24:36

place is now among the people, and he will dwell with them. They will be his people, and God himself will be with them and be their God. He will wipe every tear from their eyes. There will be no more death or mourning or crying or pain, for the old order of things has passed away.'"[69]

Satan's time is limited and his end is coming. The Death Star will be blown up, and the celebratory worship service will be awesome.

Today, as we live out our lives in Act Three, we will struggle with cancer, heart disease, depression, diabetes, and Alzheimer's. I am not the only one whose life has been marred by the death of a loved one. We all have scars. But when Jesus returns, these things will be abolished and death itself will be defeated.

Paul describes the launch of Act Four in 1 Thessalonians: "Brothers and sisters, we do not want you to be uninformed about those who sleep in death, so that you do not grieve like the rest of mankind, who have no hope. For we believe that Jesus died and rose again, and so we believe that God will bring with Jesus those who have fallen asleep in him. According to the Lord's word, we tell you that we who are still alive, who are left until the coming of the Lord, will certainly not precede those who have fallen asleep. For the Lord himself will come down from heaven, with a loud command, with the voice of the archangel and with the trumpet call of God, and the dead in Christ will rise first. After that, we who are still alive and are left will be caught up together with them in the clouds to meet the Lord in the air. And so we will be with the Lord forever. Therefore encourage one another with these words."[70]

We have a tendency to make our story arcs much too small. I typically see just my individual life as my entire story. The beginning of my story was when I was born and the end is when I die. Sometimes I see my story even smaller, revolving just around the good or bad day I am having! But it is not about me—I am part of His story.

The most fantastical moment in a story, the point when all the tension is relieved, probably won't happen during my little earthly life. My personal

---

[69] Revelation 21:3-4

[70] 1 Thessalonians 4:13-17

story doesn't climax so that everything on her side of a particular moment is made to be okay. There is no r ion to my story so that my family can live happily ever after. I will nev ıbrace Mack again until "the twinkling of an eye, at the last trumpet," w e and I will both be raised imperishable.[71]

I am learning to be okay with not knowing God allowed Mack to die when He did. God says, "Be still and know God."[72] He didn't say "Be still and know why." I can trust Him to ru Universe, and I can trust His sovereign game plan for getting us fro Three to Act Four.

No one knows when Act Four will begin, e can trust it is coming. I, personally, can't wait for when Jesus reuni , and we will live and reign forever with Him.

Until then, I will keep "living in my dash," pray I will make the most of the days I have lef hope and prayer is that the life and death of my ill inspire you to know more fully the life and ı of God's Son, so that through Him you may ence life to the full.

[71] 1 Corinthians 15:52
[72] Psalm 46:10

AFTERWARD

On June 6, 2021, hundreds of friends and family members gathered to celebrate Mack and Jesus. When Mack's dear friend Heno took to the podium to share, I couldn't help but marvel at how much Mack and Jesus had in common. Clearly, the love of Christ had rubbed off on my son, I couldn't have been more proud of him.

> Good afternoon, everyone. For those who don't know me, my name is Heno. It is a great honor that the Mumford family has asked me to share some stories and insights on Mack.
>
> So first, I'd like to share how we met. After spending a season traveling around Australia and New Zealand in 2014 with a couple of the guys here (Josh and Allen) I returned home to Branson, Missouri feeling jaded and lost. I attended Bloom Church alone one Sunday morning and as soon as I walked in, a bright, animated kid with bleached hair and tattoos wearing a tank top bee lined straight towards me. He shook my hand, introduced himself, and asked if I'd like to sit with him, which I did. As someone who sometimes struggles to feel comfortable in traditional churchy scenarios, Mack immediately put me at ease.
>
> After the service, Mack invited me out to lunch at Clockers, a little diner that became a favorite in our friend group, where we indulged in biscuits and gravy and dove straight into sharing our life stories. We learned that we both had struggled with hard teenage years, we both felt like outsiders in the Midwest, and we both found a new beginning after encountering the hopeful and mysterious love of Christ.
>
> The friendship that forged at that fateful breakfast expanded outwardly into the future, and over the next six years we shared a lot of memories filled with Mack's well-curated playlists, skateboarding in vacant lots, time spent deep in prayer, spontaneous road trips to Arkansas, conversations beneath starry skies, racing to see who could get to one hundred tattoos first and the joy of cultivating a unique and eclectic community.
>
> I, like everyone else here who knew Mack, was in a constant state of

admiration for Mack's other-worldly optimism. It was who he was. When life threw setbacks his way, whether those be wrecked cars or career opportunities that fell through, he never for a second fumbled or raised his fist to God. Instead he would collect himself and chart a new course forward.

And man, that kid had some dance moves. I don't know where he got it, but whenever the music was playing, he stopped what he was doing and had to get down.

There was a time in 2016 where I was struggling with my health and was falling behind on my bills. Mack was visiting from Oklahoma, and after hearing about my predicament, he went into our guest room where his belongings were and came out with $500. He held it out to me and said, "Here. This is what kings do. Kings share their treasure with other kings." Now, Mack may have overestimated the financial generosity of monarchs, considering that $500 was probably half Mack's 'kingdom' treasury, but, metaphors aside, that kind of generosity is as kingly as a man gets in this life.

I'd like to close with the most important thing Mack taught me: Mack always considered the unconsidered. Whether it was a house church gathering, a block party, a concert or an afternoon at a swimming hole, he was always scanning his surroundings for folks who might feel left out. Few people have the ability to open up their heart wide enough to receive a beautiful mountain peak or a shimmering sea, fewer still have the ability to receive a stranger. But that's what Mack did. He would find whoever was sidelined, and he would connect with them. He would make them laugh. He would give them the greatest gift that any of us can give, by making the invisible visible. He did the same for his friends and family. He did the same for me.

My friendship with Mack showed me that there is nothing we can do in this life to better demonstrate God's love than to allow those that we encounter to be fully seen, and despite the shortcomings that we may find, to offer a smile instead of judgement, a compliment instead of a critique, and to receive one another because we've experienced a love that's made room for us too. In a world that's cascading back into tribalism, that unites itself around what it hates, Mack shared the prophetic imagination that sees past the division and self-imposed labels that we try to define ourselves with and into our common humanity.

There is no better way I can think to honor Mack's life than to continue his legacy by imparting grace and love to the folks around us, especially those who see the world differently than us, by not letting circumstances define us and by dancing when we hear the music play.

- *Heno Head*

ABOUT THE AUTHOR

Rick and Amy have been married for 29 years and they have three sons. Their oldest son, Mack, tragically died in 2020 at the age of twenty-four. Mack's younger brother, Cooper (22), is a Transformational Entrepreneurship in Missions/Intercultural Ministry Studies Major at Bethany Global University who loves running extremely long distances. Spencer (16) is a sophomore who in 8th grade. He loves cross country, track, cheesecake, and is excited for Kansas to grant him his driver's license.

Rick is the Area Director for *Search Ministries* in Greater Kansas City. God has blessed him with the privilege of introducing people to Jesus and helping them grow in their faith for thirty-three years in California, France, Colorado, Missouri, and Kansas through various church and parachurch ministries. He loves being outside, Kansas Jayhawk basketball and authentic conversations over cups of coffee. Amy loves being a Mom, visual merchandising, and doing relational ministry alongside Rick.

Made in the USA
Coppell, TX
25 November 2021